▶ **The Best Argument against God**

DOI: 10.1057/9781137354143

Also by Graham Oppy

ONTOLOGICAL ARGUMENTS AND BELIEF IN GOD (*1996*)

PHILOSOPHICAL PERSPECTIVES ON INFINITY (*2006*)

ARGUING ABOUT GODS (*2006*)

THE HISTORY OF WESTERN PHILOSOPHY OF RELIGION (*co-edited with Nick Trakakis, 2009*)

READING PHILOSOPHY OF RELIGION (*with Michael Scott, 2010*)

A COMPANION TO PHILOSOPHY IN AUSTRALIA AND NEW ZEALAND (*co-edited with Nick Trakakis, 2010*)

THE ANTIPODEAN PHILOSOPHER VOLUME 1: Public Lectures on Philosophy in Australia and New Zealand (*co-edited with Nick Trakakis, and with Lynda Burns, Steve Gardner and Fiona Leigh, 2011*)

THE ANTIPODEAN PHILOSOPHER VOLUME 2: Interviews with Australian and New Zealand Philosophers (*co-edited with Nick Trakakis, and with Lynda Burns, Steve Gardner, Fiona Leigh and Michelle Irving, 2012*)

DOI: 10.1057/9781137354143

palgrave▶**pivot**

The Best Argument against God

Graham Oppy
Monash University, Australia

palgrave
macmillan

DOI: 10.1057/9781137354143

First published 2013 by
PALGRAVE MACMILLAN

Palgrave Macmillan in the UK is an imprint of Macmillan Publishers Limited, registered in England, company number 785998, of Houndmills, Basingstoke, Hampshire RG21 6XS.

Palgrave Macmillan in the US is a division of St Martin's Press LLC, 175 Fifth Avenue, New York, NY 10010.

Palgrave Macmillan is the global academic imprint of the above companies and has companies and representatives throughout the world.

Palgrave® and Macmillan® are registered trademarks in the United States, the United Kingdom, Europe and other countries

ISBN: 978-1-137-35415-0 EPUB
ISBN: 978-1-137-35414-3 PDF
ISBN: 978-1-137-35413-6 Hardback

This book is printed on paper suitable for recycling and made from fully managed and sustained forest sources. Logging, pulping and manufacturing processes are expected to conform to the environmental regulations of the country of origin.

A catalogue record for this book is available from the British Library.

A catalog record for this book is available from the Library of Congress.

www.palgrave.com/pivot

DOI: 10.1057/9781137354143

Contents

Preface   vi

Introduction   1

1 Preliminary Matters   4

2 Some Big Ideas   11

3 Minimal Theism and Naturalism   18

4 Standard Theism and Naturalism   67

Conclusion   87

Index   91

Preface

This book is intended to be an introduction to one of the central parts of philosophy of religion, namely, the discussion of arguments about the existence of God. Given its length, this book does not aim to provide a comprehensive introduction even to this part of philosophy of religion: rather, it assumes a particular conception of God, and develops a single argument in connection with that conception of God.

The book was written during my employment at Monash University, while I was Head of the School of Philosophical, Historical and International Studies. I am grateful to the University, and more particularly to my colleagues in the Faculty of Arts, for support that enabled me to work on the book while carrying out my other institutional duties.

As always, I could not have completed this book without the support of my immediate family: special thanks and love to Camille, Gilbert – who also provided detailed comments on my first draft – Calvin and Alfie.

DOI: 10.1057/9781137354143

Introduction

Oppy, Graham. *The Best Argument against God.*
Basingstoke: Palgrave Macmillan, 2013.
DOI: 10.1057/9781137354143.

▶

Our question is the existence of God; we shall consider this question in the context of dispute between theists – those who suppose that God exists – and naturalists – those who suppose that there is nothing supernatural. Our method will be to examine as much as we can of the relevant evidence, in order to try to determine whether theism or naturalism makes a better fit with that evidence. Because much of the putatively relevant evidence has been worked up into arguments for and against the existence of God, we shall also have cause to present and comment upon a range of those arguments.

Before we can turn to our examination of the relevant evidence, there are some preliminary matters to which we shall need to attend. First, we need to get clear about what we mean by 'theism' and 'naturalism', and by associated terms (such as 'God' and 'the natural world'). Second, we need to have a clear account of the method that we shall use in order to decide whether theism or naturalism makes a better fit with the pieces of evidence that we consider. And third, there are some big questions – about the scope of possibility, about causation and chance, about freedom and determinism, and about the objectivity of morality – upon which we shall need to make some initial comments before we can commence our investigation.

The discussion that we present suggests a novel 'cumulative' argument against the existence of God. In the end, I do *not* defend the suggested 'cumulative' argument. However, the argument is worth considering because (i) it has evident advantages over other kinds of 'cumulative' arguments that have been previously discussed, and (ii) it is, at least in my estimation, the strongest extant argument about the existence of God.

References and further reading

Useful general resources for philosophy: *Oxford Bibliographies Online* (http://oxfordbibliographiesonline.com/), the *Stanford Encyclopaedia of Philosophy* (http://plato.stanford.edu/), the *Routledge Encyclopaedia of Philosophy* (http://www.rep.routledge.com/) and the *Philosopher's Index* (http://philindex.org/).
Essential reading on arguments about the existence of God: Richard Swinburne (1979) *The Existence of God* Oxford: Clarendon; John Mackie (1982) *The Miracle of Theism* Oxford: Clarendon; and Jordan Howard Sobel (2004) *Logic and Theism* Cambridge: Cambridge

DOI: 10.1057/9781137354143

University Press. Recommended collections: William Lane Craig
and J. P. Moreland (eds) (2009) *The Blackwell Companion to Natural
Theology* Malden: Wiley-Blackwell; and William Wainwright (ed.)
(2009) *Philosophy of Religion, Volume 2* London: Routledge. For a
very different opinion about the merits of theistic arguments: Alvin
Plantinga (2007) 'Two Dozen (or so) Theistic Arguments' in D. Baker
(ed.) *Alvin Plantinga* Cambridge: Cambridge University Press, 203–27.

DOI: 10.1057/9781137354143

1

Preliminary Matters

Abstract: *We characterise theism and naturalism, and provide an account of the method that we use to provide a comparative assessment of them. In particular, we discuss theoretical virtues – simplicity, goodness of fit, explanatory breadth and predictive fruitfulness – and their role in the assessment of the comparative virtues of theories; and we also consider the role that the theoretical virtues might play in an argument for the conclusion that one theory dominates another on the available evidence. We conclude with a brief account of the properties of successful arguments.*

Keywords: argument; dominance argument; Naturalism; successful argument; Theism; theory; theoretical virtue

Oppy, Graham. *The Best Argument against God.*
Basingstoke: Palgrave Macmillan, 2013.
DOI: 10.1057/9781137354143.

DOI: 10.1057/9781137354143

Theism

Theism says that there are gods: supernatural beings or forces that have and exercise power over the natural world but that are not, in turn, under the power of any higher-ranking or more powerful category of beings or forces.

Polytheism says that there is more than one god. Many ancient religions were polytheistic: consider, for example, the pantheons of Norse, Greek and Roman gods. Contemporary indigenous religions are also often said to be polytheistic, though there is room for debate about whether, for example, ancestral spirits are properly taken to be gods.

Monotheism says that there is exactly one god: God. Judaism and Islam are uncontroversially monotheistic religions. Christianity is also typically claimed to be a monotheistic religion, even though the doctrine of the Trinity might be thought to muddy the waters a bit. There is more serious debate about whether Hinduism is polytheistic; we shall not attempt to enter into that debate here. Hereafter, by 'theism', we shall mean 'monotheism' (unless context demands a wider interpretation).

On a natural 'minimal' conception, God is the source, or ground, or originating cause of everything that can have a source, or ground, or originating cause. In particular, on this 'minimal' conception, God is the cause of the existence of the natural world, and the source or ground or origin of most – if not all – of its significant features.

On 'standard' conceptions, God possesses a range of further attributes: for example, most theists agree that God is supremely powerful ('omnipotent'), supremely wise and knowledgeable ('omniscient') and perfectly good ('omnibenevolent'). While there are puzzles that can be raised about these attributes on particular ways of filling them out – for example, 'can an omnipotent being make a rock that it is unable to lift?', 'can an omniscient being be modest?', 'can a being be both perfectly merciful and perfectly just?' – we shall not attempt to investigate those kinds of puzzles in what follows.

There are many further attributes that some theists attribute to God. Contested 'generic' attributes include, among others: simplicity, infinity, impassibility, personality, consciousness, freedom, perfection, necessity, eternity and agency. And contested 'specific' attributes include, among others: having become incarnate, having atoned for our sins, loving every human being, having performed particular miracles and so forth. In the following discussion, we restrict our attention to the 'minimal'

DOI: 10.1057/9781137354143

and 'standard' conceptions of God. There are many questions that can be raised about the attribution of further generic and specific properties to God, but we shall not attempt to canvass any of those questions here.

Naturalism

Naturalism says that causal reality is natural reality: the domain of causes is nothing more nor less than the natural world.

Atheism says that there are no gods; in consequence, atheism says that there is no God. Naturalism entails atheism: if causal reality is natural reality, then there is no (supernatural) cause of natural reality, and, in particular, there is no God. But atheism does not entail naturalism: to deny that there are gods is not to insist that causal reality is natural reality. Atheists who believe in ghosts, or demons, or pixies, are not naturalists.

Supernaturalism says that causal reality outstrips natural reality: there are supernatural causes. In consequence, theism entails supernaturalism: if God exists, then God is a supernatural cause. But supernaturalism does not entail theism: to hold that there are non-natural causes is not to insist that there is a God. Supernaturalists who believe in ghosts, or demons, or pixies, but who deny that God exists, are not theists.

This 'minimal' conception of naturalism relies on a prior understanding of the distinction between the natural and the supernatural (as did our 'minimal' conception of theism). We shall proceed on the assumption that we do understand this distinction well enough. If we come to have doubts about whether we do understand this distinction well enough, then we can return to give it more careful consideration.

'Minimal naturalism' admits of elaboration in many different – mutually inconsistent – ways. Any suitably elaborated naturalism will hold that some features of the natural world are primitive – not susceptible of further explanation – whereas other features of the natural world are fully explained in terms of those primitive features. Thus, for example, some naturalists suppose that all of the primitive features of the natural world are physical features – i.e. features that lie in the proper domain of the discipline of physics. Other naturalists suppose that there are features of the natural world – for example, the psychological states of human beings – that cannot be fully explained in terms of the fundamental physical properties. The key point to note is that all naturalists suppose that there are no supernatural causal properties – and so,

DOI: 10.1057/9781137354143

in particular, there are no fundamental supernatural causal properties. Debates between naturalists about which are the fundamental natural properties will play no role in our subsequent discussion.

Method

The main question that we wish to address is whether there is reason to prefer theism to naturalism (or vice versa). We shall begin by considering the question whether there is reason to prefer minimal theism to minimal naturalism (or vice versa). Later, we shall turn to consider the question whether there is reason to prefer standard theism to a suitably elaborated naturalism (or vice versa).

Our method will be to address, one by one, a range of considerations that have been supposed to give support to one or other of the two views under assessment. Often, the considerations in question have been encoded in arguments for one or other of the views. As we go along, we shall note the consequences of our comparative assessment of the two views, against the considerations in question, for those arguments.

There is an assumption implicit in our method. We shall be assuming that a successful argument for one or other of the views in question would be an argument that appealed to considerations that favour one of the views over the other. This seems like a pretty uncontroversial assumption.

Theoretical virtues

When we compare two views – or hypotheses, or beliefs, or theories – in order to determine which one is most favoured by certain considerations, we need to have a set of criteria that we can appeal to in carrying out our comparisons. The most significant criteria that we shall be taking into account in the coming investigation are:

(a) *Simplicity*: If everything else is equal, we should prefer the more simple theory to the less simple theory. If everything else is equal, we should prefer the theory that postulates fewer (and less complex) primitive entities. If everything else is equal, we should prefer the theory that invokes fewer (and less complex) primitive

DOI: 10.1057/9781137354143

features. If everything else is equal, we should prefer the theory that appeals to fewer (and less complex) primitive principles.

(b) *Goodness of Fit*: If everything else is equal, we should prefer the theory that makes the best fit with the data. There are complexities here. In many cases, we know that our data are imperfect: our data contain errors, or noise, or the like. The 'best fit' with the data may itself involve some kind of trade off between simplicity and what we might call 'direct fit' with the data.

(c) *Explanatory Breadth*: If everything else is equal, we should prefer the theory that explains more. There are two dimensions to this. On the one hand, all else being equal, we should prefer the theory that leaves less unexplained. (This is closely related to the idea that, if everything else is equal, we should prefer the theory that invokes fewer primitive entities and features.) On the other hand, all else being equal, we should prefer the theory that 'unifies' the wider domain of features. (Again, this is also related to the idea that, if everything else is equal, we should prefer the theory that invokes fewer primitive entities, features and principles.)

(d) *Predictive Fruitfulness*: If everything else is equal, we should prefer the theory that makes the most accurate predictions of future data. If everything else is equal, we should prefer the theory that prompts the most fruitful future inquiry – that is, the theory that suggests the more fruitful avenues for future investigation.

While these criteria are not very controversial, they are also quite limited: they do not always tell us how to proceed when we have differences along more than one dimension (so that 'everything else' is not equal). In particular, for example, these criteria give us no guidance in cases in which one theory makes a better fit with the data, but leaves more things unexplained. However, these criteria will be of use in any case in which one theory does better than another on some of these criteria, and no worse than that other theory on all of the remaining criteria.

Arguments

An argument is a collection of sentences – or thoughts, or claims, or beliefs, or propositions or what have you – one of which is identified

DOI: 10.1057/9781137354143

as the conclusion, and the rest of which are the premises. Here is an example of an argument:

1 Some things are caused. (Premise)
2 Things do not cause themselves. (Premise)
3 There are no circles of causes. (Premise)
4 There are no infinite regresses of causes. (Premise)
5 There is no more than one first cause. (Premise)
6 If there is exactly one first cause, then that first cause is God. (Premise)
7 (Hence) God exists. (Conclusion, from 1–6)

Warning: The word 'argument' is also sometimes used to denote a chain of reasoning or inference that takes you from premises to conclusions. We shall not be much interested in that sense of 'argument' in what follows. (Perhaps you can see an acceptable chain of reasoning that takes you from the premises to the conclusion in our example. A 'first cause' is something that causes other things, but that itself has no cause.)

We are interested in the role that arguments might play in debate. So, imagine that Theist and Naturalist are debating the existence of God. The conclusion of an argument that Theist might put to Naturalist will be 'God exists', or 'Probably, God exists' or 'More likely than not, God exists'; and the conclusion of an argument that Naturalist puts to Theist will be 'God does not exist' or 'Probably, God does not exist' or 'More likely than not, God does not exist'.

What properties should an argument have in order for it to count as successful? We shall suppose that there are just two. First, the conclusion of the argument should be supported by the premises: perhaps the conclusion is a logical consequence of the premises, or perhaps the conclusion is made probable by the premises, or perhaps the conclusion is made more likely than not by the premises etc. Second, the premises of the argument should all be believed by the opponent in the debate. Thus, if Naturalist is trying to convince Theist that God does not exist by appealing to an argument, then the argument in question should have as its premises only claims that Theist accepts. (The point of introducing an argument into a debate is precisely to draw explicit attention to a putative problem in the beliefs of the other person – a putative logical inconsistency, or a putative probabilistic inconsistency, or a putative explanatory inconsistency or the like. Arguments need not play any role

DOI: 10.1057/9781137354143

in debates, as debates can proceed primarily in terms of invitations to explain how certain considerations are accommodated or explained on the view held by the other side. A debater has reason to give an argument only if he or she supposes that the opponent cannot see the import of certain considerations that the opponent has already accepted or been brought to accept.)

References and further reading

On the characterisation of theism: Graham Oppy (2009) 'Gods' *Oxford Studies in Philosophy of Religion* 2, 231–50. For contrast: Jordan Howard Sobel (2004) *Logic and Theism* Cambridge: Cambridge University Press; Richard Swinburne (1979) *The Existence of God* Oxford: Clarendon.

On method and theoretical virtue: Daniel Nolan (1997) 'Quantitative Parsimony' *British Journal for Philosophy of Science* 48, 3, 329–43. For a contrasting view: Scott Shalkowski (1997) 'Theoretical Virtues and Theological Construction' *International Journal for Philosophy of Religion* 41, 71–89.

On theory of argumentation: Graham Oppy (2011) 'Über die Aussichten erfolgreicher Beweise für Theismus oder Atheismus' ('Prospects for Successful Proofs of Theism or Atheism') in Joachim Bromand und Guido Kreis (eds) *Gottesbeweise von Anselm bis Gödel (Arguments for the Existence of God from Anselm to Gödel)* Berlin: Suhrkamp Verlag. For a contrasting view: Stephen Davis (1997) *God, Reason and Theistic Proofs* Edinburgh: Edinburgh University Press.

DOI: 10.1057/9781137354143

2
Some Big Ideas

Abstract: *We provide some very brief comments on some big ideas that play a significant role in the coming argument. In particular, we consider (a) the scope of possibility and the connection between possibility and conceivability; (b) the nature of causation, and the connection between causation and chance; (c) freedom, and the relationship between freedom and causal determinism; and (d) moral responsibility, and its connections to freedom, causation, and moral objectivity.*

Keywords: causation; chance; conceivability; determinism; freedom; morality; objectivity; possibility; responsibility

Oppy, Graham. *The Best Argument against God.*
Basingstoke: Palgrave Macmillan, 2013.
DOI: 10.1057/9781137354143.

Scope of possibility

We can certainly *imagine* our world being quite different from how it actually is. We can certainly imagine, for example, a world in which we are smarter, richer and more athletic than we actually are. Furthermore, we typically suppose that the world *might have been* different from the way that it actually is. Perhaps, for example, we *might have been* smarter, richer and more athletic than we actually are.

Philosophers disagree about the scope or extent of possibility, that is, about the range of ways in which the world *might have been* different from how it actually is.

At one extreme, there are philosophers who suppose that, if you can consistently imagine the world being a certain way, then the world might have been that way. On this view, imagination is a reliable – but nonetheless fallible – guide to how things might have been: fallible only because we are not perfectly reliable in determining when our imaginings are consistent.

At the other extreme, there are philosophers who suppose that any alternative way that things might have been must have started out in the way that things actually are started out, and then departed from the way that things actually are solely as the result of some chance event. (On the most extreme version of this view, according to which there are no chance events, there is no alternative way that things might have been: everything that is the case had to be the case!)

Suppose that 'the actual world' is the complete way that things actually are. Then a 'possible world' is a complete way that things might have been. On the second of our extreme views, every possible world shares a 'common initial part' with the actual world, and departs from it only as a result of the outworkings of chance.

A step back from the second extreme view would allow that even the 'initial' part of the actual world might have been different. On this view, there are two distinct sources of alternative possibilities, that is, of alternative ways that things might have gone. First, there is the outworkings of chance. But, second, there is brute – completely uncaused and unexplainable – variation in initial conditions.

Theism admits of variations that fit both the extreme view and the step back from the extreme view. On the Theistic version of the extreme view, the initial causal state – God's existing and being disposed to make other things – could not have been other than it actually was. On the Theistic version of the step back from the extreme view, the initial causal state might have been other than it actually was – even though God could not have failed to exist – because God's initial disposition to make other things could have been other than it actually was (either because God could have failed to have an initial disposition to create, or because God could have had initial dispositions to create that differed from the particular initial dispositions to create that he actually had in the initial state). Suppose we say that something is 'contingent' just in case it might have been some other way, and that it is 'necessary' if it could not have been any other way. The preceding discussion shows that theism can say either that the initial causal state was necessary, or that the initial causal state was contingent.

Naturalism also admits of variations that fit both the extreme view and the step back from the extreme view. On the version of Naturalism that fits the extreme view, there is a necessary initial natural causal state: an initial natural causal state that could not have been other than it actually is. On the version of Naturalism that fits the step back from the extreme view, there is a contingent initial natural causal state (contingent either because the existence of the entities involved in that initial state is contingent, or because at least some of the properties of the entities involved in that initial state are contingent). If we pretend that the initial natural causal state is the initial state of 'the singularity', then it might be that the existence of the singularity is contingent, or it might be that at least some of the initial properties of the singularity are contingent. At least pending provision of reasons to the contrary, naturalism can say either that the initial causal state was necessary, or that it was contingent.

Causes and chances

Some philosophers have maintained that causal relations are the basic glue that unifies our world; other philosophers have denied that there are any causal relations at all. In the following discussion, we are going to suppose that the former philosophers are right. (If we suppose that rejecting this assumption would make a difference to the conclusions that we ultimately draw, then we can return to reconsider it.)

Think of our world as a network of causal entities (events, processes and states). When we say that there is a causal relation between two things, there are two very different broad ideas that we might have in

DOI: 10.1057/9781137354143

mind. On the one hand, we might be thinking that the cause is *sufficient* for the effect: in this case, it must be that we get the effect given that we have the cause. On the other hand, we might be thinking that the cause is *necessary* for the effect: in this case, it must be that we get the effect only if we have the cause.

The former idea supplies us with the notion of causal determinism. If causes are sufficient for their effects – and, in particular, if the laws of evolution of state combine with present states to provide sufficient causes for future states – then, given the laws and the initial state of the universe, there is only one possible way that things can go. The past causally determines the future.

The latter idea provides us with a notion of causation that implies no commitment to determinism. If causes are only causally necessary for their effects, then there is room for (objective) chances – that is, room for alternative possible ways that things could go, even given the laws and a complete initial state.

Some Theists have supposed that our world is governed by sufficient causation; however, most Theists have supposed only that our world is governed by necessary causation. (We shall discuss the reasons for this in the next section.)

Naturalists are also divided on this topic. Some naturalists suppose that our world is deterministic; many do not. In particular, there is dispute about the interpretation of quantum mechanics. Some Naturalists say that quantum mechanics establishes that our world contains objectively chancy events; other Naturalists deny this. (Naturalists are also divided on the question whether causation is necessary or sufficient for the same reason that Theists are. Again, see the next section.)

If we do think of our world as a network of causal entities, then we can speculate about the global shape of this network. There are a limited number of simple possibilities. It could be that the global network involves a regress under the causal relation: every causal entity has prior causal entities as causes. Or it could be that there is an initial entity in the global causal network: it could be that there is an entity that causes other things, but that is not itself caused. (Or it could be that there are several initial entities in the global causal network. But we shall set this last thought aside. If we decide that taking it into account would make a difference to our final conclusions, we can return to reconsider it.) And, of course, if there is an initial entity in the global causal network, then that initial entity could be necessary, or it could be contingent

DOI: 10.1057/9781137354143

(and, if it is contingent, it may or may not involve necessarily existing objects).

Freedom

Some philosophers – 'compatibilists' – have defended the view that freedom is compatible with determinism. Other philosophers – 'incompatibilists' – have denied that freedom is compatible with determinism. Incompatibilists divide into two camps: 'libertarians' – who insists that we are capable of free action, and hence who reject determinism – and 'hard determinists' – who embrace determinism, and consequently deny that we are capable of free action.

Compatibilists and incompatibilists typically disagree about what is required for free action. Compatibilists typically say something like this: that a person acts freely just in case that person acts on his or her normally acquired mental states – beliefs, desires, intentions and so forth – in the absence of certain kinds of defeating conditions (e.g. he or she is not imprisoned, not under duress, not under the influence of alcohol or other mind-altering drugs, not the victim of brainwashing and so forth). Incompatibilists typically say something like this: that a person acts freely just in case that person could have done any of a range of things in the very circumstances in which they acted.

Theists are often libertarians; and, of course, those Theists who are libertarians suppose that our world is governed only by necessary causation. Given the way that we have defined 'objective chance', libertarian free actions are objectively chancy. This is not to say that libertarian free actions are 'chancy' in some further, intuitive sense. Libertarians often suppose that libertarian free actions involve a distinctive kind of causation – 'agent causation' – in which a person (rather than an event, or process or state) is the cause of an event, or process or state. Compatibilists typically insist that this is impossible: only events, or processes, or states can stand in causal relations.

Naturalists are often compatibilists who deny that there can be libertarian free actions. However, as noted above, naturalists are also often committed to the claim that our world is governed only by necessary causation (because they have other reasons – not concerned with freedom – for supposing that there are objectively chancy events, processes and states). In our subsequent discussion, we shall nearly always suppose that we are assuming only that causes are necessary for their effects.

DOI: 10.1057/9781137354143

Morality and objectivity

One reason – among many – for caring about freedom is that we are apt to suppose that freedom is intimately connected with moral responsibility. Certainly, there seems to be fairly strong *prima facie* reason to hold that, if we do not act freely, then we are not (morally) responsible for what we do. But, of course, compatibilists and libertarians can agree that freedom is required for moral responsibility; where they disagree is on what it takes for an agent to act freely.

It is a commonplace that philosophers disagree widely about morality. Some philosophers suppose that there are (objective) moral truths and values; some philosophers do not. Some philosophers suppose that (objective) moral truths are both necessary and primitive; some philosophers do not. Some philosophers who suppose that (objective) moral truths are neither necessary nor primitive also suppose that (objective) moral truths can be given an evolutionary explanation; and other philosophers who suppose that (objective) moral truths are neither necessary nor primitive suppose that moral truths can be explained in terms of God's commandments.

There are various opinions that Theists hold about moral truth. Some suppose that it is necessary and/or primitive. But others suppose that moral truths can be explained in terms of God's commandments.

Similarly, there are various opinions that Naturalists can hold about moral truth. Some suppose that it is necessary and/or primitive. Others suppose that moral truths can be explained in evolutionary – or other naturalistic – terms. Yet others suppose that there is no moral truth (and some of those suppose that the 'illusion' of moral truth can be explained in evolutionary – or other naturalistic – terms).

In our subsequent discussion, we may need to consider reasons for adopting one or another position on these questions about moral truth. At the very least, we will need to bear in mind the full range of positions that are available to Theist and Naturalist.

References and further reading

On theories of modality: David Lewis (1986) *On the Plurality of Worlds* Oxford: Blackwell; Steve Yablo (1993) 'Is Conceivability a Guide to Possibility?' *Philosophy and Phenomenological Research* 53, 1–42; Tamar Gendler and John Hawthorne (eds) (2002) *Conceivability*

DOI: 10.1057/9781137354143

and Possibility Oxford: Oxford University Press; Timothy O'Connor (2008) *Theism and Ultimate Explanation: The Necessary Shape of Contingency* Oxford: Blackwell.

On causes and chances: John Mackie (1974) *The Cement of the Universe: A Study in Causation* Oxford: Clarendon; Judea Pearl (2000) *Causality: Models of Reasoning and Inference* Cambridge: Cambridge University Press; James Woodward (2003) *Making Things Happen: A Theory of Causal Explanation* Oxford: Oxford University Press; Toby Handfield (2012) *A Philosophical Guide to Chance* Cambridge: Cambridge University Press.

On freedom: Gary Watson (ed.) (2003) *Free Will*, second edition Oxford: Oxford University Press. (The selected bibliography at the end of *Free Will* is particularly useful.)

On morality and objectivity: John Mackie (1977) *Ethics: Inventing Right and Wrong* Harmondsworth: Penguin; Michael Smith (1994) *The Moral Problem* Oxford: Wiley-Blackwell; Richard Joyce (2001) *The Myth of Morality* Cambridge: Cambridge University Press.

DOI: 10.1057/9781137354143

3
Minimal Theism and Naturalism

Abstract: *We set out the central material of the book: a detailed comparison of the theoretical merits of Minimal Theism and Minimal Naturalism. We start with a comparison of our two theories prior to the introduction of data, and then go on to consider, in turn, global causal structure; cosmic fine-tuning; the history of the earth; the history of humanity; a priori knowledge; morality and human flourishing; consciousness and reason; religious experience; and scripture, authority, organisation and tradition. We argue that, prior to the introduction of data, naturalism trumps theism on grounds of simplicity and that none of the data that we consider favours theism over naturalism. We conclude that, given the data considered, naturalism wins.*

Keywords: Anselm; Aquinas; argument for design; cosmological argument; fine-tuning; Hume; ontological argument; Paley; religious experience

Oppy, Graham. *The Best Argument against God.* Basingstoke: Palgrave Macmillan, 2013. DOI: 10.1057/9781137354143.

DOI: 10.1057/9781137354143

We are going to compare the theoretical virtues of Minimal Theism and (Minimal) Naturalism in connection with an expanding range of considerations ('data'). We begin with a comparison prior to the introduction of any data.

"Greatest Possible Being"

Some philosophers suppose that Theism can be shown to be true by pure reason alone, without any consideration of empirical data. Those philosophers are committed to the claim that Theism can be shown to be superior to Naturalism by pure reason alone, without any consideration of empirical data.

Some (other) philosophers suppose that Naturalism can be shown to be true by pure reason alone, without any consideration of empirical data. Those philosophers are committed to the claim that Naturalism can be shown to be superior to Theism by pure reason alone, without any consideration of empirical data.

Philosophers who suppose that Naturalism can be shown to be superior to Theism by pure reason alone typically suppose either (a) that Theism involves some kind of internal contradiction, or else (b) that the greater simplicity of Naturalism is an advantage that no amount of empirical data can trump. (It is clear that Naturalism is simpler than Theism: it postulates fewer kinds of entities, fewer kinds of primitive properties and fewer kinds of primitive principles. According to Theism, there are two kinds of entities – natural and supernatural – whereas according to Naturalism, there is only one kind. According to Theism, there are two kinds of causation – natural causation and supernatural causation – whereas according to Naturalism, there is only one kind. Etc.)

It seems implausible to claim that there is some internal contradiction in the claim that God – the one and only god – is the source, or ground, or originating cause of everything that can have a source, or ground, or originating cause. But this claim is all that Minimal Theism is committed to.

It also seems implausible to claim that the greater simplicity of Naturalism gives it an advantage that no amount of empirical data could trump. At the very least, it seems that we can *imagine* obtaining data that would tell very strongly in favour of Theism. At one point in his *Dialogues Concerning Natural Religion*, David Hume (1711–76) has one of his characters ask us to imagine that a voice comes from the sky, addressing each

DOI: 10.1057/9781137354143

person on the earth in a language that that person understands, and delivering a message fit for a god. If part of the message that the voice delivered was that there is just one god, it seems plausible to suppose that we would have empirical data that *might* trump the greater simplicity of Naturalism.

Philosophers who suppose that Theism can be shown to be superior to Naturalism by pure reason alone typically suppose either (a) that Naturalism involves some kind of internal contradiction, or else (b) that there are considerations internal to Theism that guarantee its truth.

It seems implausible to claim that there is some internal contradiction in the claim that there are none but natural causes. But this claim is all that (Minimal) Naturalism is committed to.

It also seems implausible to claim that there are considerations internal to Theism that guarantee its truth. Consider the view of the (Minimal) Naturalist who holds that all possible worlds 'share an initial part' with the actual world, and diverge from it only as a result of the outworkings of objective chance. This (Minimal) Naturalist will suppose that expressions like 'the greatest possible being', 'the being than which no greater can be conceived', 'the most perfect being', and so forth, fail to denote or refer to any possible being. But, without the assumption that these kinds of expressions at least denote or refer to possible beings, it is hard to see how one can even make sense of the idea that there are considerations internal to Theism that guarantee its truth. We can illustrate the difficulties here by considering the most famous example of an argument that attempts to establish that considerations internal to Theism guarantee its truth.

Anselm's Proslogion II argument

St. Anselm of Canterbury (1033–1109) produced the following argument (of course, what is given here is a translation from his Medieval Latin):

> Even the fool is convinced that a thing than which no greater thing can be thought is in the understanding, since when he hears this – ['a thing than which no greater thing can be thought'] – he understands it; and whatever is understood is in the understanding. And certainly a thing than which no greater thing can be thought cannot be in the understanding alone. For if it is even in the understanding alone, it can be thought to exist in reality also, which is greater. Thus, if a thing than which no greater thing can be thought is in the understanding alone, then a thing than which no greater thing can be thought is itself a thing than which a greater thing can be

DOI: 10.1057/9781137354143

thought. But surely this cannot be. Thus without doubt a thing that which no greater thing can be thought exists both in the understanding and in reality. (*Proslogium; Monologium; an Appendix in Behalf of the Fool; and Cur Deus Homo*, translated by Norton Deane, Chicago: Open Court, 1903, 7–8)

This is a fascinating argument, though perhaps a little difficult to get your head around at first. Anselm's key idea is that the assumption that a thing than which no greater thing can be thought exists only in the understanding – and not also in reality – leads to a contradictory conclusion. Given that it is contradictory to claim that a thing than which no greater thing can be thought exists only in the understanding, and given that a thing than which no greater thing can be thought does exist in the understanding, it certainly seems to follow that a thing than which no greater thing can be thought exists in reality. Moreover, you might think, there is surely something to the idea that it is greater to exist in reality than it is to exist merely in the understanding: how could a thing than which no greater thing can be thought *be thought* to exist only in the understanding? Finally, if a thing than which no greater thing can be thought exists in reality, then it seems plausible to suppose that that thing is the sole creator of everything else, omnipotent, omniscient, perfectly good and so on – in other words, it seems plausible to suppose that, if there is a thing than which no greater thing can be thought, then that thing is God.

Despite all of this, it seems that there is a straightforward argument to the conclusion that Anselm's argument cannot be good. This counter-argument – or something very much like it – was first advanced by a contemporary of Anselm, a monk known as 'Gaunilo', in 1079. Gaunilo observed that, if Anselm's argument were good, then the following argument – against a 'fool' who denied that there is in reality an island than which no greater island can be thought – would also be good:

> Even the fool is convinced that an island than which no greater island can be thought is in the understanding, since when he hears this – ['an island than which no greater island can be thought'] – he understands it; and whatever is understood is in the understanding. And certainly an island than which no greater island can be thought cannot be in the understanding alone. For if it is even in the understanding alone, it can be thought to exist in reality also, which is greater. Thus, if an island than which no greater island can be thought is in the understanding alone, then an island than which no greater island can be thought is itself an island than which a greater island can be thought. But surely this cannot be. Thus without

DOI: 10.1057/9781137354143

doubt an island that which no greater island can be thought exists both in the understanding and in reality.

The crucial point here is that the chain of reasoning is exactly the same in the two cases: if the conclusion follows in Anselm's argument, then the conclusion also follows in Gaunilo's parody. But the conclusion of Gaunilo's parody is obviously mistaken: no one seriously supposes that there is, in reality, an island than which no greater island can be thought. (And, of course, there is nothing special about islands. A variant of Gaunilo's parody can be run for any kind of thing that admits of comparison in terms of better and worse. Do you think that there is, in reality, a footballer than which no greater footballer can be thought?)

Perhaps it might be objected that the assumptions in Anselm's argument are more plausible than the assumptions in Gaunilo's parody. But what are these assumptions?

First, we have the assumptions that the expressions 'being than which no greater being can be thought' and 'island than which no greater island can be thought' are understood when heard. Perhaps you might try saying: there is an intrinsic maximum of greatness for beings, but not for islands (or anything else). That is, in the case of 'being', we really can think of a maximal being: a being that is omnipotent, omniscient, perfectly good and so forth. But in the case of 'island', we cannot really think of a maximal island: for any island that we can think of, we can think of a greater one – one with more coconut palms, and lagoons, and so forth. However, this is not very convincing. On the one hand, it seems that no being can be maximal along all dimensions: for example, nothing can be maximally merciful and maximally just. And, on the other hand, if there were an island than which no greater island can be thought, it would be one in which there was an optimal trade-off between the various great-making features of an island: it would not be too big, nor too crowded with trees, nor too much filled in with water and so forth. Considerations about intrinsic maximality do not give us reason to think that only one of the expressions is understood when heard.

Second, we have the assumptions that it is greater for a being than which no greater being can be thought to exist in reality than to exist only in the understanding and that it is greater for an island than which no greater island can be thought to exist in reality than to exist only in the understanding. It is, I think, very hard to come up with any cogent reason for thinking that one of these assumptions is more plausible than the other.

DOI: 10.1057/9781137354143

But there are no other assumptions in Anselm's argument. So, it seems, Gaunilo's objection is decisive. Of course, you might wonder whether there is some way of reformulating Anselm's argument so that it avoids Gaunilo's objection without becoming subject to some other serious liability. I think that no one has yet succeeded in doing this. However, you might not want to take my word for this. And, in any case, it might be that further investigation will turn up such an argument.

Be all of this as it may, there is a further reason for suspicion of Anselm's argument. Consider how things look from the standpoint of Naturalist. As we noted earlier, according to Naturalist, the expression 'that than which no greater can be conceived' almost certainly fails to refer to any possible being. But, if this expression fails to refer to a possible being, then the assumption that it refers to something in the understanding entails that there are impossible things in the understanding. And if there are impossible things in the understanding, then there is no barrier to its being true in our understanding that an island than which no greater island can be thought is itself an island than which a greater island can be thought! In order to be entitled to run arguments by *reductio ad absurdum*, you must not be tolerant of impossibilities: but Anselm's argument can't even get started unless it is granted that 'that than which no greater can be conceived' refers to a possible being; and this is something that Naturalist need not – and indeed will not – be prepared to grant.

Global causal structure

The first piece of data that we introduce is the observation that there is a global causal structure: the world is a network of causal relations. One of the standard philosophical questions is, 'why is there something rather than nothing?' In the present context, we interpret this question to mean, 'why is there causal stuff, rather than complete absence of causal stuff?'

How Naturalist answers this question depends upon the view that Naturalist takes of the scope of possibility. If Naturalist supposes that every possible world 'shares an initial part' with the actual world, then Naturalist can say: it was impossible for there to be complete absence of causal stuff. In other words: there is causal stuff because there had to be causal stuff. If Naturalist has a more relaxed view of the scope of

DOI: 10.1057/9781137354143

possibilities – and, in particular, if Naturalist supposes that it is possible that there might have been no causal stuff – then Naturalist will say: there is no reason why there is causal stuff rather than complete absence of causal stuff – it is just a brute fact that there is causal stuff.

How Theist answers this question depends upon the view that Theist takes of the scope of possibility. If Theist suppose that every possible world is one in which God engages in causal activity, then Theist can say: it was impossible for there to be complete absence of causal stuff. In other words: there is causal stuff because there had to be causal stuff. If Theist has a more relaxed view of the scope of possibilities – and, in particular, if Theist supposes that it is possible that God might have engaged in no causal activity – then Theist will say: there is no reason why there is causal stuff rather than complete absence of causal stuff – it is just a brute fact that there is causal stuff.

Given that Naturalist and Theist have exactly the same options when it comes to explaining why there is causal stuff rather than complete absence of causal stuff – each can hold that it is necessary that there is causal stuff, and each can hold that it is a brute fact that there is causal stuff – considerations about global causal structure do not count in favour of one view rather than the other.

The conclusion that we have reached here may be surprising to some readers. After all, cosmological arguments are widely recognised to be among the strongest standard arguments for the existence of God – and yet cosmological arguments typically appeal to considerations about global causal structure. However, we can illustrate the strength of our conclusion through consideration of one of the classic cosmological arguments.

Aquinas' Second Way

In the second half of the 13th century, in his *Summa Theologiae* – First Part, Second Question, Third Article – St. Thomas Aquinas gives the following argument:

The second way is based on the nature of causation. In the observable world, causes are found to be ordered in series; we never observe, nor ever could, something causing itself. ...Such a series must however stop somewhere. ... One is therefore forced to suppose some first cause, to which everyone gives the name 'God'. (*Summa Theologiae*, Volume 2, translated by T. McDermott, Eyre and Spottiswoode, 1964)

DOI: 10.1057/9781137354143

Setting aside worries about the conception of causation that is operative in Aquinas' argument, we note that the text provides a ballpark approximation to the generic causal argument that we mentioned in our earlier discussion:

1 Some things are caused. (Premise)
2 Things do not cause themselves. (Premise)
3 There are no circles of causes. (Premise)
4 There are no infinite regresses of causes. (Premise)
5 There is no more than one first cause. (Premise)
6 If there is exactly one first cause, then that first cause is God. (Premise)
7 (Hence) God exists. (Conclusion, from 1–6)

(There are some extra premises in the generic argument that are not present in Aquinas' argument. Can you see why these extra premises have been included?)

What will Naturalist say about this argument? Well, whether or not Naturalist is inclined to dispute any of the other premises, it is clear that Naturalist will not assent to the sixth premise. According to Naturalist, if there is exactly one first cause, then that first cause is the initial (causal) state of natural reality, that is, the first cause is something that is natural (and hence not a god). Naturalist might also have doubts about some of the other premises – for example, the third, the fourth, and the fifth – but we do not need to assess those premises before we arrive at the conclusion that this argument cannot possibly provide a reason to favour Theism over Naturalism.

The point that we have just made is closely related to two standard general criticisms of cosmological arguments. (These are not just criticisms of the particular argument from Aquinas that we have chosen to examine). The first point is that it seems implausible to suppose that mere considerations about the shape of the global causal order can establish that some part of that global causal order is supernatural. This point is sometimes obscured because proponents of cosmological arguments assume that all of the natural causal order is contingent – but, as we have seen, that assumption is not mandatory for Naturalists (any more than it is mandatory for Theists to suppose that all of the causal order – natural and supernatural – is contingent). The second point is that, while it is wrong to think that the question 'Who made God?' raises a serious problem for Theism – after all, Theist supposes that God is,

DOI: 10.1057/9781137354143

or is intimately involved in, the first cause – there is a serious problem for proponents of cosmological arguments that arises with the question 'From whence came the causal order?' Once we focus our attention on the global causal order – and not on the question whether the natural causal order itself has a cause – we see clearly that considerations about the shape of the global causal order do not differentially support either Theism or Naturalism.

That these criticisms do have wider currency can be brought out by consideration of other well-known cosmological arguments. Consider, first, the kalām cosmological syllogism:

1 Everything that begins to exist has a cause of its existence.
2 The universe [= the natural causal order] began to exist.
3 (Therefore) The universe [= the natural causal order] has a cause of its existence.

What shall a proponent of this argument say about the global causal order? Does it begin to exist? Because Naturalist supposes that the global causal order just is the natural causal order, Naturalist can say: if the global causal order began to exist, then it cannot have – and so does not need – a cause (whence the natural causal order cannot have – and so does not need – a cause, and the first premise of the kalām cosmological syllogism is just false); and if the global causal order did not begin to exist, then the natural causal order did not begin to exist, and so the second premise in the kalām cosmological syllogism is just false. When we consider the matter from the proper perspective, it is obvious that the kalām cosmological syllogism provides no reason at all to favour Theism over Naturalism.

Consider, second, a standard version of a cosmological argument from contingency:

1 All wholly contingent structures have causes.
2 The universe [= the natural causal order] is a wholly contingent structure.
3 (Therefore) The universe [= the natural causal order] has a cause.

What shall a proponent of this argument say about the global causal order? Is it wholly contingent? As Naturalist supposes that the global causal order just is the natural causal order, Naturalist can say: if the global causal order is wholly contingent, then it cannot have – and so does not need – a cause (whence the natural causal order cannot have – and so

DOI: 10.1057/9781137354143

does not need – a cause, and the first premise in the argument is plainly false); and if the global causal order is not wholly contingent, then the natural causal order is not wholly contingent, and the second premise in the argument is plainly false. When we consider the matter from the proper perspective, it is obvious that our cosmological argument from contingency provides no reason at all to favour Theism over Naturalism.

Cosmic fine-tuning

The second piece of data that we introduce is the (alleged) cosmic fine-tuning of the visible universe. The core idea here is that tiny variations in the values of cosmic parameters that characterise our universe would have greatly altered the history of our universe: either it would have been very short-lived – on the order of a second or less – or else it would have blown apart so rapidly that it would always have consisted of more or less nothing but empty space. But, in these 'altered' histories of our universe, it is clear that there would be no human beings, or intelligent life, or embodied agents, or carbon-based life, or, indeed self-organising complex systems of any kind at all. And that consideration might be taken to prompt the following question: 'Why do the cosmic parameters that characterise our universe take the values that they do?'

For the purposes of the ensuing discussion, we shall assume that it is simply true that tiny variations in the values of cosmic parameters that characterise our universe would have greatly altered the history of our universe in the way described. Some cosmologists do not accept that this is so; some others say that the appearance of cosmic fine-tuning is only an artefact of our currently inadequate cosmological models. But, on the other hand, there are many cosmologists who suppose that cosmic fine-tuning is already a firmly established fact concerning the visible universe.

Let us first consider how things appear from the standpoint of Naturalist. If Naturalist supposes that every possible world 'shares an initial part' with the actual world, and if Naturalist also supposes that there is no part of the actual world at which the values of the relevant cosmic parameters vary, then Naturalist will (inevitably) suppose that the values of the cosmic parameters are necessary: the values of the cosmic parameters could not have been other than they actually are! (In the remainder of our discussion, we shall simply assume that there is no part of the actual world at which the values of the relevant cosmic parameters vary.

DOI: 10.1057/9781137354143

If we find reason to suppose that it might be that there are parts of the actual world at which the values of the relevant cosmic parameters vary, then we can return to consider the consequences of this supposition.)

If Naturalist does not suppose that every possible world 'shares an initial part' with the actual world, then Naturalist will be free to suppose that the relevant cosmic parameters might have always had values different from the values that they actually have. In that case, it seems, Naturalist would need to suppose that it is simply a brute fact that the relevant cosmic parameters take the values that they do: ultimately, there is no explanation why the relevant cosmic parameters take the values that they do. Whether this would be problematic for Naturalist is a point to which we shall return.

Let us now consider how things appear from the standpoint of Theist. If Theist supposes that every possible world 'shares an initial part' with the actual world, then either (a) Theist will suppose that there is an objectively chancy connection between God's initial state and God's making of the initial state of our universe, or else (b) Theist will suppose that it is necessary that God made the initial state of our universe. If it is necessary that God made the initial state of our universe that actually obtained, then the values of the relevant cosmic parameters are necessary: the values of the cosmic parameters could not have been other than they actually are! On the other hand, if there is an objectively chancy connection between God's initial state and God's making of the initial state of our universe, then it seems that it is simply a brute fact that the relevant cosmic parameters take the values that they do (rather than other values that they might have taken).

If Theist does not suppose that every possible world 'shares an initial part' with the actual world, we still have the same two possibilities concerning the connection between God's initial state and God's making of the initial state of our universe. On the one hand, if this connection is objectively chancy, and if God's initial state is brutely contingent, then it is simply a brute fact that the relevant cosmic parameters take the values that they do (rather than other values that they might have taken). On the other hand, if the connection is necessary, the fact that God's initial state is brutely contingent still entails that it is simply a brute fact that the relevant cosmic parameters take the values that they do (rather than other values that they might have taken).

Given that Theist and Naturalist have exactly the same options when it comes to explaining why the cosmic parameters that characterise our

DOI: 10.1057/9781137354143

universe take the values that they do – each can hold that it is necessary that those cosmic parameters take the values that they do, and each can hold that it is brutely contingent that those cosmic parameters take the values that they do – it seems that we should conclude that considerations about the values of those cosmic parameters do not favour one of those views above the other.

The conclusion that we have just suggested will doubtless seem wrong to some readers. After all, the reason why the fine-tuning of the cosmic parameters has seemed significant to many Theists is precisely because it seems that the fine-tuning of the cosmic parameters might be explained in terms of God's *choosing* values for the cosmic parameters in such a way as to ensure that – or, at any rate, make it possible for – human beings, or intelligent life, or embodied agents, or carbon-based life, or self-organising complex systems of some kind to come into existence.

There might be something to this objection. The crucial question overlooked in the preceding discussion concerns the range of values that the cosmic parameters might have taken in the two scenarios. If we suppose that Naturalist would have to allow that there is a greater range of values that the cosmic parameters might have taken than Theist would allow, then perhaps we should allow that the position of Theist is more strongly supported by the evidence. But why should we suppose that Naturalist would have to allow that there is a greater range of values that the cosmic parameters might have taken than Theist would allow? That just seems like an arbitrary stipulation. And yet, if we are comparing: (i) a view that says that it is a brute fact that parameters take a value from a given range, with (ii) a view that says that parameters were chosen to take a value from the same range, but it is simply a brute fact that this particular choice was made – it is very hard to see why we should think that one view affords a more satisfying explanation than the other.

Could God have chosen to make a universe that lasts for less than a second? Could God have chosen to make a universe that blows apart so rapidly that it is mostly empty space? If we suppose that the answer to either of these questions is affirmative, then we cannot also say that God *must* have all-things-considered reason to prefer a 'life-permitting' universe to one of these 'non-life-permitting' alternatives. But, if God needn't have all-things-considered reason to prefer a 'life-permitting' universe to one of these 'non-life-permitting' alternatives, then, on the assumption that God's *choosing* is a brute fact, it surely does turn out that

DOI: 10.1057/9781137354143

Theist has no better explanation than Naturalist of why it is that relevant cosmic parameters take the values that they do.

History of the Earth

The third piece of data that we introduce is the accumulated body of knowledge about the nature and history of the earth, including, in particular, the accumulated body of knowledge about the nature and history of living organisms. There are two questions that we shall consider in connection with this data. The first question is whether the content of well-established astrophysics, geology, geophysics, geochemistry, physical geography, palaeontology, biology, biochemistry, physiology, microbiology, genetics, ecology, pharmacology and so forth, favours Theism over Naturalism (or vice versa). The second question is whether the existence of complex living organisms and complex ecological systems favours Theism over Naturalism (or vice versa).

Some might be inclined to think that the content of the accumulated body of 'natural science' is bound to favour Naturalism over Theism. In particular, some might think to draw attention to the fact that there is not one single well-established result in the 'natural sciences' that depends upon the postulation of the existence of God. There is no established knowledge in astrophysics, or geology, or geophysics, or geochemistry, or palaeontology, or biology, or biochemistry, or physiology, or microbiology, or genetics, or ecology, or pharmacology, or any other of the 'natural sciences' that relies upon the assumption that God exists. If one looks in textbooks supported by the leading scientific academies of the world, one looks in vain for the words 'We begin by supposing that God exists and is the source, or ground, or originating cause of everything that can have a source, or ground, or originating cause'. On the basis of these kinds of considerations, we could pretend that Laplace was speaking for 'natural scientists' in general when he purportedly said 'We have no need for that hypothesis'.

However, it seems to me that it would be a mistake to suppose that these considerations somehow show that the content of the accumulated body of 'natural science' supports Naturalism over Theism. Rather, it seems to me that the content of the accumulated body of well-established 'natural science' has no implications at all for the dispute between Naturalist and Theist: there just is no reason why Theist *must* suppose that the existence

DOI: 10.1057/9781137354143

of God has implications for the content of the 'natural sciences'. (Theist can perfectly well suppose that natural science is our *only* reliable source of information about the natural world that God created.)

Some people will think that the claims that I have just made cannot possibly be correct. In particular, there are many Theists who suppose that the existence of complex living organisms and their complex parts – eyes, brains, flagella, etc. – provides strong differential support for Theism over Naturalism. On the one hand, there are Theists who suppose that 'natural science' gives an incomplete explanation of the existence of complex living organisms and their complex parts (even though the given explanation is fine as far as it goes); on the other hand, there are Theists who suppose that the explanation that 'natural science' gives of the existence of complex living organisms and their complex parts is both incomplete *and* erroneous in the details that it actually supplies.

Theists who suppose that 'natural science' gives a merely incomplete explanation of the existence of complex living organisms and their complex parts suppose that God's creative decisions stand at the beginning of the causal series of events that leads eventually to the natural world as we currently see it: God chose initial conditions and laws that ensured – or, at least made it likely – that human beings, or intelligent life, or embodied agents, or carbon-based life, or self-organising complex systems of some kind would eventually appear in our universe. As we have already discussed this view in the preceding section (on cosmic fine-tuning), we need not give it further consideration here.

Theists who suppose that 'natural science' gives a *mistaken* explanation of the existence of complex living organisms and their complex parts typically oppose or reject parts of the accumulated body of 'natural science'. In particular, such Theists typically deny that evolutionary theory provides even a partial explanation of the existence of human beings, human eyes, human brains, bacterial flagella and the like. However, given the theoretical values against which we are assessing the dispute between Naturalist and Theist, it seems that we are obliged to see this as a win for Naturalist: after all, there is no working alternative biological theory that provides the same level of simplicity, predictive accuracy, goodness of fit and explanatory breadth that is afforded by evolutionary theory. (Perhaps this verdict might be overturned when we bring in further evidence about scripture, authority and tradition; we should bear this point in mind when we turn to consider further evidence.)

DOI: 10.1057/9781137354143

Theists who suppose that 'natural science' gives a mistaken explanation of the existence of complex living organisms and their complex
parts are often supporters of (biological) teleological (design) arguments
for the existence of God. We conclude our discussion in this section with
an examination of the most famous biological design argument for the
existence of God.

Paley's 'Watch' argument

In 1805, in his *Natural Theology*, William Paley writes as follows:

> [W]hen we come to inspect [a] watch ... the inference, we think, is inevi-
> table; that the watch must have had a maker. ... [Yet] every manifestation
> of design, which existed in the watch, exists in the works of nature; with
> the difference, on the side of nature, of being greater and more, and that in
> a degree which exceeds all computation. (*Natural Theology, American Tract
> Society*, 1881, 9–10)

Clearly, we can agree with Paley that, when we observe a watch, we do
'inevitably' suppose that the watch has a maker. Moreover, as Paley notes,
we would 'inevitably' make this supposition even if we had never seen a
watch before, had no idea what the function of a watch is, had only a
broken or malfunctioning watch before us and so forth. But why is this?
What is it about watches that makes it 'inevitable' that they should have
this effect upon us?

Paley claims that, when we observe the watch, we see that it has a
principal function, that its parts have functions and that the materials
from which the watch and its parts are constructed are well suited to the
functions that those parts have. Moreover, Paley claims that it is because
we see *these* things that we 'inevitably' form the view that the watch has
a maker.

Paley's claims are implausible. Consider the real-life example of the
discovery of the antikythera mechanism in 1900–1901. The discoverers
of this mechanism immediately recognised that it was a man-made
artefact, even though they had no idea about its principal function, nor
about the sub-functions served by the parts, nor (consequently) whether
the materials from which the mechanism and its parts were constructed
were well suited to the functions in question. (Recent investigation
has established that the antikythera mechanism is actually an ancient
mechanical computer designed to calculate the positions of significant
astronomical objects: the sun, the moon, the planets and the stars. But it

DOI: 10.1057/9781137354143

was more than 50 years from the discovery of the antikythera mechanism before anyone came close to figuring this out.)

How is it, then, that those who found the antikythera mechanism were immediately able to identify it as a man-made artefact? Well, they could see immediately that it was composed from metals that do not occur in nature – for example, bronze. They could see immediately that it has a shape that does not belong to the natural world. They could see immediately that there were cog-wheels in its interior – and, of course, they knew full well that cog-wheels do not grow on trees. Etc.

These points are utterly destructive of Paley's argument. When we observe plants and animals, we do NOT find them to be composed of metals that are not found in nature. When we observe plants and animals, we do NOT find them to have shapes that do not belong to the natural world. When we open up plants and animals, we do NOT find that they contain cog-wheels. Etc. In other words, it is simply false that '*every* manifestation of design, which existed in the watch, exists in the works of nature'.

Perhaps it might be objected that, even if Paley is wrong about how we actually discern that something is an artefact, he is nonetheless right that considerations about function and suitability of constitution to function suffice to establish that something is an artefact. Even if it isn't true that we recognise that a watch is an artefact by discerning its function, and observing that its material constitution is suited to its function, isn't it still the case that we could recognise that an object is an artefact simply by discerning its function and noting that its material constitution is suited to its function?

No, that's also plainly not correct. Consider, for example, a rabbit's heart – perhaps Paley has one on his dissection bench. There is no doubt that the rabbit's heart belongs to a kind that has a function, and that its material constitution is suited to that function – but there is also no doubt that there is nothing 'inevitable' about the supposition that the rabbit's heart is an artefact. While Theist may believe that rabbit's hearts are artefacts – because designed by God – there is no question that Naturalist has not the slightest inclination to agree. And, of course, Naturalist supposes that there is an alternative, evolutionary explanation of the presence in the world of rabbit's hearts (with the functions, and suitability of material constitution to functioning that we observe them to have).

The upshot of this discussion is clear: Paley's argument provides no reason at all to prefer Theism to Naturalism. Moreover, the difficulty that

DOI: 10.1057/9781137354143

we have highlighted for Paley's argument has some generality: there are many contemporary versions of arguments for biological design that falter over exactly the same kinds of considerations. Consider, for example, the 'irreducible complexity' variant of Paley's argument that has been defended by Michael Behe. According to Behe, inferences to design are 'inevitable' when we detect 'irreducible complexity' – roughly, when we observe that something is (a) composed of several well-matched interacting parts that contribute to its basic function, and (b) such that the removal of any one of the parts causes it to effectively cease functioning. Consider, for example, a common mousetrap: if any of the wooden platform, or the spring with extended ends, or the hammer, or the holding bar, or the catch is missing, then the mousetrap stops functioning altogether (whence, by Behe's definition, the common mousetrap is irreducibly complex).

The idea that it is detection of irreducible complexity that underwrites our ability to identify artefacts is no more plausible than Paley's suggestion that it is detection of function and suitability of material constitution to function that underwrites this ability. (We could identify mousetraps as artefacts even if we had no idea what function they were intended to serve, and even if it never occurred to us that mousetraps are irreducibly complex.) But, even if we agree that we do not *need* to identify the presence of irreducible complexity in order to establish that something is an artefact, perhaps we might nonetheless suppose that, wherever we find irreducible complexity, we do then find intelligent design? Surely not! I would stop functioning if you removed my brain, or my heart, or my lungs, etc: whence it follows that I am irreducibly complex. But it is simply absurd to suppose that *this* consideration alone suffices to establish that Naturalist does not have – and cannot have – an evolutionary explanation of the presence in the world of human brains, human hearts, human lungs and so forth. (If it were *that* easy to show that evolutionary theory is mistaken, then you can be quite sure that serious scientists – for example, the kind that belong to the world's major scientific academies – would long since have abandoned it.)

History of humanity

The fourth piece of evidence that we shall consider is the accumulated body of knowledge about the nature and history of human beings and

DOI: 10.1057/9781137354143

human societies. There are two questions that we shall consider in connection with this data. The first question is whether the content of well-established archaeology, anthropology, ethnography, human geography, sociology, psychology, cognitive science, economics, political science, criminology, linguistics, education, international relations, legal studies, human history, communication studies and so forth favours Theism over Naturalism (or vice versa). The second question is whether the existence and nature of reports of miracles – and of other kinds of exercise of supernatural powers – over the range of human history favours Theism over Naturalism (or vice versa).

Some might be inclined to think that the content of the accumulated body of 'social science' is bound to favour Naturalism over Theism. In particular, some might think to draw attention to the fact that there is not one single well-established result in the 'social sciences' that depends upon the postulation of the existence of God. There is no established knowledge in archaeology, or anthropology, or ethnography, or human geography, or sociology, or psychology, or cognitive science, or economics, or political science, or criminology, or linguistics, or education, or international relations, or legal studies, or human history, or communication studies, or any other of the 'social sciences' that relies upon the assumption that God exists. If one looks in textbooks supported by the leading social scientific academies of the world, one looks in vain for the words 'We begin by supposing that God exists, and is the source, or ground, or originating cause of everything that can have a source, or ground, or originating cause'. On the basis of these kinds of considerations, we could pretend that Laplace was speaking for 'social scientists' in general when he purportedly said 'We have no need for that hypothesis'.

However, as I noted in my earlier discussion of the 'natural sciences', it seems to me that it would be a mistake to suppose that these kinds of considerations show that the content of the accumulated body of 'social science' supports Naturalism over Theism. Rather, it seems to me that the content of the accumulated body of well-established 'social science' has no implications at all for the dispute between Naturalist and Theist: there is just no reason why Theist *must* suppose that the existence of God has implications for the content of the 'social sciences'. (After all, Theist can perfectly well suppose that 'social science' is our only reliable source of information about the 'social world' that God created.)

Some people will think that the claims that I have just made cannot possibly be correct. In particular, there are many Theists who suppose

DOI: 10.1057/9781137354143

that there are phenomena that lie within the domain of human history that are much better explained on the hypothesis that God exists than on the hypothesis that causal reality is natural reality. In particular, there are many Theists who suppose that there are events from recorded human history – miracles – that are best understood to be results of direct intervention by God in the natural causal order. While Naturalists suppose that the best explanations of reports of miracles – or reports of experiences of the miraculous – can always be framed within the confines of 'naturalistic social sciences' or naturalistic discourse more broadly construed, some Theists suppose that the best explanations for at least some reports of miracles – or reports of experiences of the miraculous – advert to the direct intervention by God in the natural causal order.

There are countless reports of miracles across the world's religions. Consider, for example, the well-known reports concerning: Buddha's painless birth (and conception without sexual intercourse); Arunagirinathar's survival after he threw himself from a temple tower; Jesus' turning of water into wine; Mohammed's splitting of the moon; the shaking of the earth, the darkening of the sun, and the raining of beautiful flowers from the sky consequent upon the execution of Ichadon by King Beopheung of Silla; Sarkar Waris Pak's wading across the flooded Ghanghra river; the regrowth of Miguel Juan Pellicer's amputated leg; the sun's dimming, changing colours, spinning, dancing about in the sky and plummeting to the earth at Fátima; the healing powers of Audrey Marie Santo; and so on.

There are also countless reports of other kinds of *anomalous* interventions, episodes, activities and phenomena in the course of human history. Consider, for example, reports concerning: astrological influences, alien (extraterrestrial) visitations, channelling, clairvoyance, cryptids (e.g. bunyips, hoop snakes, Loch Ness monsters, man-eating trees, mermaids, werewolves, will-o'-the-wisps and yeti), demons, dowsing, ESP (extrasensory perception), fairies, fortune-telling, ghosts, goblins, out-of-body experiences, prophecy, reincarnation, telekinesis, telepathy and witchcraft; and consider, too, the vast range of reports emanating from practices that can be collected together under the heading of 'alternative medicine' or 'spiritual healing' (e.g. Bach flower remedies, chiropractic, chromotherapy, crystal healing, cupping, ear candling, homeopathy, iridology, magnotherapy, naturopathy, reflexology, reiki, rolfing and so forth).

Of course, while the truth of some of the further reports just mentioned would (arguably) be inconsistent with Naturalism, the truth of others would not. However, when we come to assess the evidential import of

DOI: 10.1057/9781137354143

reports of miracles for the dispute between Theist and Naturalist, we need to consider the full range of reports of interventions, episodes, activities and phenomena that are anomalous from the standpoint of currently well-established science. It is uncontroversial that the truth of pretty much everything referred to in the preceding two paragraphs has not been confirmed by natural and social scientific investigation. It is also uncontroversial that the domain of investigation of these kinds of interventions, episodes, activities and phenomena is ripe with 'knavery and folly' (as David Hume says in his famous discussion of miracles). The upshot for those who would claim that some particular reports of miracles are evidence for Theism over Naturalism is clear: we need to be given some very good reason to suppose that these particular reports have truth-relevant features that clearly distinguish them from the vast body of reports concerning the miraculous and the anomalous. In the absence of very good reason to suppose that the particular reports in question have truth-relevant features that clearly distinguish them from the vast body of reports concerning the miraculous and the anomalous, the evidently proper conclusion to draw is that the particular reports in question offer no serious support for Theism over Naturalism.

Our discussion to this point leaves it open whether there *are* particular reports of miracles that have truth-relevant features that clearly distinguish them from the vast body of reports concerning the miraculous and the anomalous. Hume was in no doubt on this matter:

> [T]here is not to be found, in all history, any miracle attested by a sufficient number of men, of such unquestioned good sense, education and learning, as to secure us against all delusion in themselves; of such undoubted integrity, as to place them beyond all suspicion of any design to deceive others; of such credit and reputation in the eyes of mankind, as to have a great deal to lose in case of their being detected in any falsehood; and at the same time, attesting facts performed in such a public manner and in so celebrated a part of the world, as to render the detection unavoidable. (*Enquiries concerning Human Understanding and concerning the Principles of Morals*, edited by L. A. Selby-Bigge and revised by P. H. Nidditch, Oxford: Clarendon, 1975, 116–7)

It seems to me that, if we only take account of the evidence that we have considered to this point – global causal order, cosmic fine-tuning, large-scale history and human history – then we should agree with Hume: as we haven't yet found anything *else* that favours Theism over Naturalism, we should suppose that taking account of the *full* body of reports concerning

DOI: 10.1057/9781137354143

the miraculous and the anomalous also does not favour Theism over Naturalism. However, if we subsequently discover *other* considerations that do favour Theism over Naturalism, then perhaps we might have reason to reconsider this judgment. Pending future considerations, then, we should conclude that there is nothing in considerations about global causal order, cosmic fine-tuning and the accumulated knowledge of the 'natural sciences' and the 'social sciences' that favours Theism over Naturalism, and perhaps considerations about global causal order, cosmic fine-tuning and the accumulated knowledge of the 'natural sciences' and the 'social sciences' favour Naturalism over Theism.

A priori knowledge

The fifth piece of evidence that we shall consider is the accumulated body of *a priori* knowledge: knowledge of mathematics, logic, statistics and the like. (We might argue about what else should be counted as belonging to the accumulated body of *a priori* knowledge. Perhaps there is at least some knowledge of metaphysics that is *a priori*. Perhaps there is at least some knowledge of modality that is *a priori*. Perhaps there is least some other knowledge in philosophy that is *a priori*. We shall not need to concern ourselves with the exact compass of *a priori* knowledge in our subsequent discussion.)

Some theists – for example, René Descartes (1596–1650) – suppose that God has established the truth of those things that we know *a priori*: God has established the truths of mathematics, and the truths of statistics, and the truths of logic, and the truths of metaphysics, and so forth. However, this seems wrong. If it is true that God has *established* the truths of mathematics, and the truths of statistics, and the truths of logic, and the truths of metaphysics, then there is a point in the global causal order at which this establishment occurs: there is some initial part of the global causal order in which the truths of mathematics, and the truths of statistics, and the truths of logic, and the truths of metaphysics do not obtain; and then, consequent upon God's creative work, it comes about that the truths of mathematics, and the truths of statistics, and the truths of logic, and the truths of metaphysics do obtain. But now ask yourself: what is true of the global causal order prior to the establishment of the truths of mathematics, and the truths of statistics, and the truths of logic, and the truths of metaphysics? Surely, if God exists, God is identical to

DOI: 10.1057/9781137354143

God at all parts in the global causal order. Surely, if God exists, God is one – or perhaps three! – at all parts in the global causal order. Surely, if God exists, God is not a mere abstract particular at any point in the global causal order. But these claims can be true only if there are truths of mathematics, and truths of statistics, and truths of logic, and truths of metaphysics at *all* parts in the global causal order.

Perhaps one might think to say: even though God has established the truths of mathematics, and the truths of statistics, and the truths of logic, and the truths of metaphysics, they are nonetheless true at all points in the causal order. But this can't be right! In the causal order, causes are *prior* to their effects. To say that something has been established by something else is immediately to commit oneself to the claim that the latter thing is causally prior to the former – and that can be so only if there is some way that the former thing is prior to its bringing about the latter. In other words, the truths of mathematics, and the truths of statistics, and the truths of logic, and the truths of metaphysics cannot be causally derivative necessities. Moreover, even if the truths of mathematics, and the truths of statistics, and the truths of logic, and the truths of metaphysics could be causally derivative necessities, these truths could not possibly be 'established' as the result of the libertarian free choices of an agent, because the libertarian free choices of an agent cannot be (derivatively causally) necessary. Hence, even if – *per impossible* – one could have a view on which the truths of mathematics, and the truths of statistics, and the truths of logic, and the truths of metaphysics, were 'established' by God, the ultimate source of these truths would lie beyond God, in whatever it was that causally determined God to 'establish' these truths.

Even if it is agreed that Theism has no advantage over Naturalism when it comes to the provision of truthmakers for mathematics, statistics, logic, metaphysics and the like – that is, even if it is agreed that Theism has no advantage over Naturalism when it comes to the explanation of the *truth* of the claims of mathematics, statistics, logic, metaphysics and the like – it might still be possible to argue that Theism does have an advantage over Naturalism when it comes to explaining how it is that we have *knowledge* of (some of) the truths of mathematics, statistics, logic, metaphysics and so forth. In particular, Theist might claim that it is only because God has so constituted us that we are able to know those truths of mathematics, statistics, logic, metaphysics and so forth, that we in fact know.

This claim may appear incredible. Surely we can come to knowledge of at least some of the truths of mathematics, statistics, logic and

DOI: 10.1057/9781137354143

metaphysics through the testimony of – or through training and education by – others; and it seems plausible that these considerations offer no
advantage to Theism over Naturalism. Moreover, there are direct ways
in which we can come to knowledge of at least some of the truths of
mathematics, statistics, logic and metaphysics that also seem to offer no
advantage to Theism over Naturalism.

Consider the mathematical claim – first proven by Euclid – that there
are infinitely many prime numbers. How do we know that this claim
true? Well, we can prove it in the following way. Suppose that it were
false. In that case, there would be only finitely many prime numbers, and,
at least in principle, we could give a complete list of them. Now, consider
the number that you obtain by first multiplying together all of the prime
numbers on our (finite) list and then adding one. This new number
cannot possibly be divisible (without remainder) by any of the prime
numbers on our list. (If you add 1 to a number that is divisible by 2, then
you get a number that is not divisible by 2. If you add 1 to a number that
is divisible by 3, then you get a number that is not divisible by 3. Etc. As
the number that you obtain by multiplying all of the numbers on our list
is – obviously! – divisible by each of the numbers on our list, the number
that you get by adding one to the number that you obtain by multiplying all of the numbers on our list is – obviously – not divisible by any
of the numbers on our list.) So, either our new number is prime (which
contradicts our assumption that we had made a list that contains all of the
prime numbers), or else our new number has prime factors that are not
on our list (and this, too, contradicts our assumption that we had made
a list that contains all of the prime numbers). So the claim that there are
only finitely many prime numbers leads to contradiction, whence we can
conclude that there are, indeed, infinitely many prime numbers.

Given that there is no evident reason why this kind of mathematical
proof is more challenging for Naturalist than it is for Theist, we need to
look elsewhere for support for the idea that we need to invoke God in
order to explain our knowledge of (some of) the truths of mathematics, or logic, or statistics, or metaphysics. Perhaps the thought might be
something like this: if we suppose that there is a domain of things – the
numbers – that make true the claims of arithmetic, then, from the
standpoint of Naturalist, it is utterly mysterious how we come to have
knowledge about the things in that domain. In particular, it seems that
Naturalist is committed to denying that we can have causal interaction
with the things in that domain: after all, numbers are not constituents of

things in the natural causal order. But, if Naturalist does deny that we can interact causally with the numbers, then what account could Naturalist possibly give of our knowledge of them?

At this point, Naturalist might seek to turn the tables: what account could Theist possibly give of our knowledge of the numbers, given that we have no causal contact with them? Perhaps Theist might be inclined to suppose that we have a non-natural mental faculty – 'intuition' – that does put us into causal contact with the numbers; but it is not, I think, credible to suppose that our knowledge of mathematics depends upon our being in causal contact with numbers and other non-natural mathematical objects. Opinion amongst contemporary philosophers of mathematics is divided. On the one hand, there are nominalists, fiction-alists and structuralists who deny that there is a domain of things – the numbers – that make true the claims of arithmetic. On the other hand, there are Platonists who, while accepting that there is a domain of things – the numbers – that make true the claims of arithmetic, deny that our knowledge of mathematics depends upon our being in causal contact with the members of that domain (typically holding, instead, that the existence of numbers can be *inferred* from other features of our best global theories). If we are guided by the range of positions that is taken seriously in contemporary philosophy of mathematics, then we shall suppose that considerations about our knowledge of mathematics do not differentially support either Theist or Naturalist.

Perhaps there is one last way in which we might try to make out the claim that Theism has an advantage over Naturalism when it comes to explaining how it is that we have *knowledge* of (some of) the truths of mathematics, statistics, logic, metaphysics and so forth. In particular, it might be supposed that Theist has an advantage when it comes to the explanation of knowledge of fundamental principles that can be known *a priori* – and, in particular, when it comes to the explanation of our knowledge of fundamental *logical* principles that can be known *a priori*.

Lewis Carroll's entertaining fragment of dialogue 'What the Tortoise Said to Achilles' (*Mind* 4, 14, 1895, 278–80) might be taken to establish the following point: if someone fails to see that a certain inference is logically required, then it may well be impossible to convince them that the infer-ence in question is logically required. Suppose that you cannot see that from 'A' and 'If A then B' it follows that 'B'. Clearly, it will be pointless for me to suppose that you ought nonetheless to be able to see that it follows from 'A' and 'If A then B' and 'If A, and if A then B, then B' that 'B'. After

DOI: 10.1057/9781137354143

all, the very same cognitive skill is required in the drawing of the second inference that was required in the drawing of the first. Moreover, it is not implausible that any argument that I might try to give to persuade you of the acceptability of the former inference will itself need to make use of an inference of the very kind about which you are in doubt.

Suppose that the kinds of considerations just advanced persuade you that it is simply impossible to provide a logical justification for the acceptance of basic logical principles. Then perhaps you will suppose that it seems plausible that there can be no justification for the acceptance of some basic logical principles. Rather, it seems that, in order to be a logical reasoner, it must be that you are simply 'programmed' to accept certain basic logical principles (or basic patterns of logical reasoning). But then, Theist might say, isn't it the case that you need to appeal to God in order to explain why it is that human beings are (by and large) 'programmed' to accept certain basic logical principles (and certain basic patterns of logical reasoning)?

It is to be expected that Naturalist will demur. As a softening up exercise, consider the results of the experiments reported by Wolfgang Kohler in *The Mentality of Apes* (1925). Kohler suspended bananas well beyond the reach of his chimpanzees. He found that his chimpanzees could assemble two sticks together to make a single instrument, pile up some boxes and then use the assembled instrument from the top of the boxes to pull down the bananas. Given Kohler's account, it is hard to resist the suggestion that chimpanzees are 'programmed' to accept certain basic patterns of logical reasoning. But, on the supposition that there are good evolutionary reasons why chimpanzees are thus 'programmed', it is hard to resist the further thought that there are bound to be good evolutionary reasons why human beings are also 'programmed' to accept certain basic patterns of logical reasoning. And, certainly, creatures that were 'programmed' to accept certain basic patterns of illogical reasoning, or that were not 'programmed' to accept the basic patterns of logical reasoning displayed by Kohler's chimpanzees, would be less likely to flourish in the kinds of environments that are to be found on our planet.

We have found no reason at all, then, to suppose that adding the accumulated body of *a priori* knowledge to the evidence that we had previously considered – global causal order, cosmic fine-tuning and the accumulated knowledge of the 'natural sciences' and the 'social sciences' – does anything to pull back the initial advantage that Naturalism has over Theism.

DOI: 10.1057/9781137354143

Morality and human flourishing

The sixth piece of evidence that we shall consider is the domain of morality and human flourishing. There are a number of questions here to which we shall turn our attention. Does the existence of moral truths favour Theism over Naturalism? Does our possession of moral knowledge favour Theism over Naturalism? Does the phenomenon of moral conscience favour Theism over Naturalism? Is Theism favoured over Naturalism because Theism conduces to moral virtue? Is Theism favoured over Naturalism because Theistic belief polices moral behaviour? Is Theism favoured over Naturalism because Theism conduces to happiness?

Moral truth

We have already noted that that there are various different positions open to Theist and Naturalist on the question of moral truth. Some philosophers suppose that moral truth is necessary and/or primitive. Some philosophers suppose that moral truth is explicable (e.g. in terms of evolutionary history or in terms of divine commands). Yet other philosophers suppose that there is no such thing as moral truth: morality is illusory, or subjective, or primarily concerned with desire rather than belief, etc.

The view that moral truth is necessary and/or primitive is available to both Theist and Naturalist: it provides the same explanatory advantages and incurs the same theoretical costs in each case. If we suppose that this is the most attractive view of moral truth, then, of course, we shall suppose that considerations about moral truth afford no advantage to either Theist or Naturalist.

The view that God establishes moral claims faces an immediate difficulty that is of exactly the same kind as the difficulties that confront that claim that God establishes the truths of mathematics, or logic, or statistics, or metaphysics, or the like. If it is true that God *establishes* the truths of morality, then there is a point in the global causal order in which the truths of morality do not obtain, and then, consequent upon God's creative work, it comes about that the truths of morality obtain. But now ask yourself: what is true of the global causal order prior to the establishment of the truths of morality? Surely, if God exists, God is good – and just, and loving – at all points in the causal order. And yet this can be so only if there are some moral truths that hold at all points in the global causal order.

DOI: 10.1057/9781137354143

Of course, the claim that there are some moral truths that hold at all points in the global causal order is consistent with the further claim that some moral truths are established by God. The point being made here is not that it is impossible for there to be moral truths that depend upon God's commands; rather, the point being made here is that it is impossible for it to be the case that God has moral properties only as a causal consequence of God's own commands, that is, only as a result of God's *establishing* fundamental moral truths. (Perhaps we might also think to argue in the following way. If it were true that it was up to God to establish fundamental moral truths by divine fiat, what would be the range of moral truths that God could have established? Could it have been, for example, that murder, rape, lying, stealing and cheating were good because God proclaimed them so? Surely not! But what could explain God's inability to bring it about, that murder, rape, lying, stealing and cheating are good by proclaiming them so, other than its being the case that murder, rape, lying, stealing and cheating are wrong quite apart from any proclamations that God might make? This line of thought – which is at least hinted at in Plato's dialogue *Euthyphro* – suggests that there are further reasons for supposing that at least some of God's proclamations must track independent moral truth, if the content of those proclamations is indeed true.)

The view that moral truth is explicable in terms of evolutionary history – or, more broadly, in terms that are acceptable to Naturalist – faces similar difficulties to those that confront divine command theory. Suppose we grant that evolutionary history – or other features of the history of the natural causal order – establish moral truths. What, then, should we say about the range of moral truths that could have been established by evolutionary history, or other features of the history of the natural causal order? Could it have been, for example, that evolutionary history – or other features of the history of the natural causal order – brought it about that murder, rape, lying, stealing and cheating were right and good? Surely not! But what could explain this fact other than its being the case that murder, rape, lying, stealing and cheating are wrong quite apart from our evolutionary history or any other features of the natural causal order?

While there is more to be said about the prospects for explaining moral truth, the foregoing considerations do something to suggest that, if there are explanations of moral truth, those explanations are unlikely to advantage either Theist or Naturalist.

DOI: 10.1057/9781137354143

The view that that there is no such thing as moral truth – that morality is illusory, or subjective, or primarily concerned with desire rather than belief, or etc. – is one that few Theists accept. However, insofar as we are concerned only with Minimal Theism, it is not clear that we should suppose that this view would favour Naturalism over Theism. Minimal Theism makes no assumptions about the moral properties of God, and so is perfectly consistent with the view that there is no such thing as moral truth. On the other hand, Standard Theism involves the claim that God is (necessarily) perfectly good. And, obviously enough, the claim that God is perfectly good does not sit comfortably with the view that there is no such thing as moral truth. Once we widen the range of assumptions that Theist makes, it seems that we shall have to suppose that the view that there is no such thing as moral truth does favour Naturalism over Theism.

In sum, then, considerations about moral truth may favour Naturalist over Theist on an expanded conception of God; but, so long as we restrict our attention to Minimal Theism, it seems that considerations about moral truth offer no advantage to either Theist or Naturalist.

Moral knowledge

Given that it is contentious whether there are moral truths, it is equally contentious whether there is moral knowledge. As we have just seen, if there are no moral truths – and hence there is no moral knowledge – then *this* is some reason to prefer Naturalism to Standard Theism (but not, I think, reason to prefer Naturalism to Minimal Theism). On the other hand, if there is moral knowledge, then there is moral truth – and, as we have just seen, if there is moral truth, then it is plausible that moral truth is necessary (and that some of it is theoretically primitive). But, if moral truth is necessary (and/or theoretically primitive), then our assessment will follow exactly the same path as our assessment of mathematical knowledge, logical knowledge, statistical knowledge, metaphysical knowledge, philosophical knowledge and so forth. In sum, then: considerations about moral knowledge provide no reason to prefer Minimal Theism to Naturalism (or vice versa), but there being no moral knowledge would plausibly favour Naturalism over Standard Theism.

Conscience

Most people are familiar with the phenomena of conscience: we feel guilt, remorse and shame when we commit actions that go against our

DOI: 10.1057/9781137354143

moral values – even if no one else discovers that we have so acted – and we feel righteous and justified when our actions conform to our moral values – again, even if no one else observes our actions. Is there reason to suppose that these facts about our moral psychology favour Theism over Naturalism (or vice versa)?

Theist might argue: the feelings of conscience are best understood in terms of agents looking beyond themselves towards a supernatural being who is witness to their actions, and before whom it is appropriate to have the feelings that they do. On this way of understanding the matter, the phenomena of conscience show that *normal* people are all at least implicitly committed to the idea that there is *always* someone who observes what we do, and before whom it is appropriate to respond as we do – and hence, to the idea that *normal* people are all at least implicitly committed to the rejection of Naturalism.

Naturalist might respond: it is true that feelings of conscience are best understood in terms of agents looking beyond themselves, but there is no reason to suppose that all people take themselves to be looking towards a supernatural being who is witness to their actions, and before whom it is appropriate to have the feelings that they do. Rather, what agents take themselves to be looking towards is the *demands* that are made upon them by others – in the first instance, the demands of friends and family, and, more broadly, the demands of society and its institutions and traditions. If I have done something that goes against moral values that I share with my friends, family and society at large, it seems that nothing more is needed to explain why I feel guilty, or remorseful, or ashamed, even if no one else is witness to my deed.

The upshot here seems to be this: if all else is equal, then Theist and Naturalist can both satisfactorily accommodate or explain the phenomena of conscience, that is, the phenomena of conscience provides no reason to favour Theism over Naturalism (or vice versa). However, if nothing else has outweighed the greater initial theoretical virtue of Naturalism, then we should continue to prefer Naturalism to Theism (on account of that greater initial theoretical virtue).

Virtue

Often, proponents of particular religions claim that followers of the religion in question are morally superior to those who do not belong to that

DOI: 10.1057/9781137354143

religion. Often enough, people who suppose that moral virtue is more abundantly attached to members of particular religions also suppose that this fact is evidence of the truth of the claims of the religion in question. Might Theist plausibly claim that, as Theism conduces to virtue, this is a reason to prefer Theism to Naturalism?

How might we decide whether it is true that Theism is more conducive to virtue than Naturalism? Well, we can compare societal data from countries with a higher percentage of Theists (and a lower percentage of Naturalists) to countries with a lower percentage of Theists (and a higher percentage of Naturalists). If Theism really does conduce more to virtue than Naturalism does, then we should surely see patterns in the societal data that reveal greater virtue in countries with a higher percentage of Theists and a lower percentage of Naturalists.

Consider, then, the data in the following table (taken from www. nationmaster.com):

	Ireland	US	Australia	Denmark
Weekly Church Goers	84%	44%	16%	5%
Abortion (per 'average woman' over lifetime)	0.18 (estimated from recorded Irish abortions performed in England)	0.69	0.57	0.48
Burglary (per capita)	1.98	0.714	1.530	1.318
Murder (per 100,000)	1.3	9.1	1.2	1.1
Rape (per capita)	0.4	0.4	1.0	0.4
Suicide (per 100,000)	2.2	2.2	2.1	2.2
Assault (per 100,000)	2.4	1.2	2.4	1.2
Divorce (per 1,000)	0.83	4.45	2.52	2.81
Imprisonment (per 100,000)	0.99	7.15	1.16	0.72
Teen Birth Rate (per 1000 girls)	not recorded	64	21	10
Below Poverty Line	5%	12 %	4 %	12 %
Obesity (per capita)	13%	31 %	22 %	10 %
Smoking (daily)	25 %	17.5 %	19.8 %	28 %
Alcohol (litres/year)	13.5	8.3	9.8	11.5
Software Piracy (as % of all software used)	not recorded	20%	28%	25%

DOI: 10.1057/9781137354143

The kind of comparative data represented in this table has to be handled with care. Often, different countries use different methods and standards when collecting and reporting data. Often, even in countries that try hard to collect accurate data, the figures are known to be approximate at best. Often, there are delicate issues involved in interpreting the data even when the same people use the same methods to collect the data across different countries. Etc.

However, what we see in this table is what we see in every set of data of this kind that I have seen – for example, in the data presented in standard demographical textbooks, or in the data presented in the *Britannica Year Book*, or in the data presented in *Wikipedia*, and so on – namely, that there is nothing in the data that supports the claim that increased national religiosity is correlated with increased national virtue. When we look at a broad range of indicators of personal and societal dysfunction, countries with relatively low levels of religiosity – such as Denmark and Australia – do not score worse than countries with relatively high levels of religiosity – such as Ireland and the United States.

Perhaps Theist might object that religious belief is itself a particularly important constituent of moral virtue. However – aside from the evidently self-serving nature of this suggestion – the crucial point to note is the curious independence of this alleged moral virtue from uncontroversial moral virtues. Even if we are not given to supposing that there is a unity to virtue – so that there is at least some correlation between the exhibition of one virtue and the exhibition of other virtues – we should surely find it strange that something that is alleged to be a particularly important constituent of moral virtue fails to be significantly correlated with uncontroversial measures of societal dysfunction (murder rates, rape rates, burglary rates, alcohol abuse rates, drug abuse rates, marital breakdown rates, teen pregnancy rates and so forth).

Perhaps Theist might appeal to personal experience. On the one hand, Theist knows lots of fellow believers who are paragons of virtue. On the other hand, the 'naturalists' that Theist knows about – Madalyn Murray O'Hair, Josef Stalin, Bertrand Russell and so on – are, if not evidently vicious, certainly people of much lesser moral standing. Of course, Naturalist can make a very similar appeal. On the one hand, Naturalist knows lots of fellow unbelievers who are paragons of virtue. On the other hand, the 'theists' that come most readily to mind – Ted Haggard, Jimmy Swaggart, John Geoghan and so on – are, if not evidently vicious, certainly people of much lesser moral standing.

DOI: 10.1057/9781137354143

There is a familiar phenomenon at work here: *cognitive bias*. We are very good at paying attention to – and absorbing – information that confirms our firmly entrenched opinions and stereotypes; we are much less good at paying attention to – and absorbing – information that conflicts with our firmly entrenched opinions and stereotypes. (No doubt, this is only part of the story. Often we do not know whether people are 'theists', or 'naturalists', or something else again. And the sub-communities to which we belong may well be constituted in such a way that we rarely come into contact with those who are – or who we know are – members of 'other' groups: 'theist', 'naturalist' or whatever.)

The upshot here is obvious. On the one hand, there is nothing in the data about societal dysfunction that confirms the superior moral virtue of Theists or Naturalists. On the other hand, we have a ready explanation of why the parties to our dispute may mistakenly think that, nonetheless, moral virtue is unevenly distributed in their favour.

Might Naturalist object that, in fact, social data actually shows that there is a correlation between lack of religiosity and moral virtue? After all, apart from the national data concerning societal dysfunction, there is also data that seems to show, for example, that naturalists are, *on average*, less likely to turn up in US prisons. But there is also data that seems to show that, *on average*, naturalists are smarter and better-educated wherever they are found – and, of course, it is not at all surprising that, within the boundaries of any given nation, there is a positive correlation between, on the one hand, intelligence and education, and, on the other hand, decreased levels of societal dysfunction.

While there is clearly much more work to do in this area, it seems to me that we should be wary of supposing that either Naturalist or Theist is in a position to claim a greater share of moral virtue, simply in virtue of their espousal of Naturalism or Theism. Moreover, and even more clearly, we should be very wary of supposing that, because a greater share of moral virtue attaches to one or other of these positions, we have evidence that one of these positions is to be preferred to the other.

Enforcement

Often, proponents of particular religions claim that their religious beliefs are all that stand between them and a life of vice and illegality. Theist might say: were it not for my belief in God, I would be killing, and looting, and maiming, and leading a life of utter licence and debauchery.

DOI: 10.1057/9781137354143

Theist might also say: the same goes for everyone else: we would all be killing, and looting, and maiming, and leading lives of utter licence and debauchery were it not for the fact that my religious beliefs are sufficiently widespread. Belief in God is all that stands between us and savagery: our society is erected on the foundations of that belief, and is imperilled as that belief is imperilled.

Naturalist should not take any of this seriously. If Theist is right in claiming that, but for his belief in God, he would be killing, and looting, and maiming, and leading a life of utter licence and debauchery, then Naturalist might (a) be relieved that Theist has the beliefs in question but (b) be worried that he has such slight protection in the event that Theist loses those beliefs. However, it is doubtless evident that Naturalist will also simply suppose that Theist is *self-deceived*: fortunately for almost everyone else, Theist would *not* be killing, and looting, and maiming, and leading a life of utter licence and debauchery if he were to lose his religious beliefs. In particular, Naturalist can reflect on the data concerning societal dysfunction that we considered in the previous section: the evidence we have simply does not support the view that 'naturalists' are more likely than 'theists' to go in for killing, and looting, and maiming, and leading lives of utter licence and debauchery.

Perhaps Theist might object that it is Naturalist who is self-deceived: Naturalist may have successfully internalised sanctions against killing, and looting, and maiming, and licence and debauchery, but (a) those sanctions derive entirely from religious teachings, and (b) the internalisation of those sanctions cannot possibly be given any 'naturalistic' justification.

Naturalist should reply that it is not plausible to suppose that our internalised sanctions against killing, and looting, and maiming, and licence and debauchery, *derive* from religious teachings. Rather, it is much more plausible that there is an evolutionary basis for our primitive moral judgments: either the cognitive structures that deliver our primitive moral judgments were directly selected, or else the cognitive structures that deliver our primitive moral judgments are an evolutionary by-product of cognitive structures that were directly selected. It is, after all, easy to see that sanctions against killing, and looting, and maiming, and licence and debauchery, would confer selectional advantage on groups that had internalised them. Moreover, and in consequence, it is much more plausible to suppose that religious teachings arose, at least in part, as a response to those primitive moral judgings that issued from

DOI: 10.1057/9781137354143

evolutionarily selected cognitive structures – the proper direction of explanation is precisely the other way around.

Plainly enough, if Naturalist is right, then the question of justifying the internalisation of the sanctions in question does not arise: you might as well try to justify the coming in of the tide. Of course, there remains a question about the justification of the sanctions themselves – but we have already addressed that issue in our discussion of moral truth and moral knowledge, and so do not need to go over it again here.

The upshot of this discussion is that considerations about propensity to killing, and looting, and maiming, and licence and debauchery, do not favour Theism over Naturalism. Whether these considerations might favour Naturalism over Theism is something that we shall come back to when we consider the bearing of moral evil on Standard Theism in our next chapter.

Happiness

Often, proponents of particular religions claim that the devotees of those religions are happier than other people, and they sometimes go on to claim that this is a reason for supposing that the religion in question is true. In particular, there are many theists who claim – on the basis of social scientific studies – that there is quite a bit of evidence that bears out the claim that theists are happier than non-theists. Might Theist reasonably claim that the greater happiness of theists is a reason to prefer Theism to Naturalism?

It is, I think, very hard to believe that adopting Minimal Theism in preference to (Minimal) Naturalism makes – or even could make – a significant contribution to happiness. In fact, it seems hard to believe that adopting Standard Theism rather than Naturalism makes – or even could make – a significant contribution to happiness. If there is anything to the idea that theists are happier than non-theists, it would surely be tied to further beliefs about the next life, the meting out of perfect justice and so forth – that is, it would be tied to beliefs that go well beyond mere belief in the existence (and goodness) of God.

But is it really true that theists are happier than non-theists? It is certainly true that there are numerous studies in which religious believers *report* greater levels of happiness than religious non-believers. However, self-reports of levels of happiness do not constitute the sole body of evidence that bears on the assessment of levels of happiness. In particular, when we reflect on the fact that religious beliefs – about the next life,

DOI: 10.1057/9781137354143

the meting out of perfect justice and so forth – might well give religious believers a *motive* for reporting that they are particularly happy, we would do well to ask whether there is other evidence about levels of happiness that fails to align with self-report.

And, of course, there is. We have already seen some of this evidence in our discussion of moral virtue. Look again at the table that plots religiosity against societal dysfunction. If happiness is correlated with religiosity, but religiosity is not correlated with lower levels of societal dysfunction – or is perhaps even correlated with higher levels of societal dysfunction – then happiness is not correlated with lower levels of societal dysfunction – and is perhaps even correlated with higher levels of societal dysfunction. But is it absurd to suppose that happiness is not correlated with lower levels of societal dysfunction – and perhaps even correlated with higher levels of societal dysfunction. We all know that divorce, and murder, and obesity, and so forth are correlated with *unhappiness* – and so we all know that, when we take the total evidence into account, we simply do not have unequivocal evidence that religious believers are happier than religious non-believers (let alone that theists are happier than non-theists, let alone that Theist is happier than Naturalist).

In sum: we have found no reason to suppose that adding data about morality – moral truth, moral knowledge, conscience, the distribution of virtue, the enforcement of moral behaviour and the distribution of human happiness – to the evidence that we had previously considered – global causal order, cosmic fine-tuning, the accumulated knowledge of the 'natural sciences' and the 'social sciences', and the accumulated body of a priori knowledge – does anything to pull back the initial advantage that Naturalism has over Theism.

Consciousness and reason

The seventh piece of evidence that we shall consider is the domain of the mental powers and faculties of human beings. On the one hand, we shall consider our subjective conscious experience – what it is like for us to taste vegemite, or see the colour red, or hear a G-major chord played on an acoustic guitar, or feel tickles on the soles of our feet, and so forth. And, on the other hand, we shall consider our capacity to engage in explicit mathematical and logical reasoning.

DOI: 10.1057/9781137354143

Consciousness and states of mind

Human beings can become infected with rat lungworm by eating raw snails or vegetables that have been contaminated by snails. Rat lungworm larvae are transported by the blood to the brain, where they can cause permanent brain damage.

Imagine that you are a rat lungworm larva, and that you have arrived in your host's brain. As you burrow around in there, will you encounter the beliefs, desires and emotions of your host? Will you be able to recognise your host's perceptions and sensations as you pass through the neural tissue?

Some philosophers have supposed that the obviously correct negative answer to these questions is evidence in favour of theism over naturalism. On their view, this kind of thought experiment makes it clear that we suppose that our minds have a non-physical – indeed, non-natural – composition: our beliefs, and desires, and emotions, and perceptions, and sensations are not to be found in our brains, but rather in non-physical substances – our souls – that interact causally with our brains. Thus, for example, Leibniz:

> Supposing there were a machine so constructed as to think, feel, and have perception, we could conceive of it as enlarged and yet preserving the same proportions, so that we might enter it as a mill. And this granted, we should only find on visiting it, pieces which push one against another, but never anything by which to explain a perception. This must be sought, therefore, in the simple substance and not in the composite or in the machine. (*Monadology 17,* in P. Weiner (ed.) *Leibniz Selections,* New York: Charles Scribner's Sons, 1979, 536)

It is obvious that Leibniz's inference is too quick. If we suppose that our beliefs, and desires, and emotions, and perceptions, and sensations are to be found in our brains, we shall surely suppose that they are *states* or *processes* – in particular, neuro-chemical states or processes – that a worm might disrupt as it burrows through the brain, but which are certainly not *things* that it could bump into or observe. However there are other, more recent, thought experiments that many suppose provide much stronger evidence in favour of theism over naturalism.

Consider zombies. Not the animated corpses of horror fiction, but the subjectively underprivileged creatures introduced into philosophy by David Chalmers. According to Chalmers' conception, your *zombie twin* would be someone who is physically exactly the same as you – someone

DOI: 10.1057/9781137354143

with exactly the same neural states and processes going on in his or her brain – but who is entirely lacking in subjective conscious experience. If your zombie twin is possible – if it is possible that there be someone who has exactly the same neural states and processes going on in his or her brain as those that are going on in your brain, but without anything even remotely like the subjective conscious experience that you have – then it cannot be that your subjective conscious experiences are neuro-chemical states or processes. But surely you can imagine having a zombie twin!

One obvious response to this line of thought is that, actually, your zombie twin is not possible. As your subjective conscious experiences just are neuro-chemical states and processes, anyone who has exactly the same neural states and processes going on in his or her brain as those that are going on in your brain will have the same subjective conscious experiences that you have. Perhaps you can *imagine* having a zombie twin, but all that this establishes is that you are able to imagine things that are impossible. And, of course, if your subjective conscious experiences just are neuro-chemical states and processes, then your subjective conscious experiences provide no support for theism over naturalism. (Perhaps it might be said: if your subjective conscious experiences just are neuro-chemical states and processes, then isn't that evidence in favour of naturalism? After all, no one supposes that neuro-chemical states and processes can occur in a supernatural entity! But there is nothing in the preceding discussion that rules out the possibility that supernatural entities have subjective conscious experiences that are not neuro-chemical states and processes. If you suppose that androids or aliens might have subjective conscious experiences, then you can surely maintain that your subjective conscious experiences are just neuro-chemical states, while also allowing that other beings might have subjective conscious experiences that are not just neuro-chemical states. At the very least, we need some further argument to show that the supposition that our subjective conscious experiences are just neuro-chemical states favours naturalism over theism.)

But what if your zombie twin is possible? What if subjective con-scious experiences are not identifiable with neuro-chemical states and processes? What if it turns out Leibniz was right, and our subjective conscious experiences occur in our non-physical souls? Would our subjective conscious experiences then be evidence that favoured theism over naturalism?

Clearly, if we suppose that non-physical souls are non-natural, then the hypothesis that there are non-physical souls is inconsistent with

DOI: 10.1057/9781137354143

naturalism. If our subjective conscious experiences are good evidence for the existence of non-physical souls, then our subjective conscious experience does differentially support theism over naturalism. However, in that case, there is a revision of the naturalist position – call it that naturalist* position – for which this conclusion will not hold.

We are comparing two views about global causal reality. On one view – the naturalist* view – global causal reality includes two different kinds of natural* causal entities: physical entities (such as brains) and non-physical entities (such as souls) that interact causally with one another. On the other view – the theist view – global causal reality includes everything that is included in the naturalist* view, and more besides: for, apart from the natural* world there is also the supernatural domain that is inhabited by God and whatever other supernatural entities there might be. As the theist view has commitments that the naturalist* view does not, we can have reason to prefer the theist view to the naturalist* view only if there is explanatory advantage in adopting the theist view.

Perhaps it might be said: there is an advantage on the theist view, as it has the resources to explain the presence of consciousness in global causal reality! But that's not right! On the theist view, consciousness is a primitive property of God, and the connection between it and the other properties that God possesses is also primitive. Moreover, if we think of God as a substance, then the connection between consciousness and the divine substance is one further, unexplained theoretical primitive. On the naturalist* view, consciousness is a primitive property of souls, and the connection between it and the other properties that souls possess is primitive. Moreover, if we think of souls as substances, then the connection between consciousness and souls is one further, unexplained theoretical primitive. Wherein lies the advantage to one side or the other?

Perhaps it might be said: there is an advantage on the theist view, as it has the resources to explain the causal connection between brains and souls! But that's also not right! On the one hand, the naturalist* can claim that souls are *caused* to come into existence by brains achieving the right level of functioning, souls continue to interact causally with brains that have the right level of functioning, and souls are *caused* to go out of existence by brains ceasing to have that level of functioning. On the other hand, the theist can agree that this is how things work (but add that God does some extra causing to establish the causal laws that underwrite this system), or the theist can say that God establishes – that is, *causes* – causal connections between brains and souls (and this because of God's beliefs, desires, intentions, plans and so forth). In each case, the ultimate explanation might be necessary – perhaps it is necessary that properly functioning brains cause souls to come into existence, etc., and perhaps it is necessary that God has the beliefs, desires, intentions, plans and so forth that lead God to establish causal connections between brains and souls – or it might be contingent – perhaps it is contingent that properly functioning brains cause souls to come into existence, etc., and perhaps it is contingent that God has the beliefs, desires, intentions, plans, and so forth that lead God to establish causal connections between brains and souls. However the cards are played, there is no advantage to theism that emerges, even on the supposition that our subjective conscious experiences occur in our non-physical souls.

Perhaps it might be said: the preceding argument relies on the assumption that our souls cannot exist in independence from – or in the absence of – our brains. But we have evidence – from near-death experiences, out-of-body experiences, communication with the dead and so forth – that our souls can exist in independence from – or in the absence of – our brains. This evidence – the evidence from near-death experiences, out-of-body experiences, communication with the dead and so forth – does differentially support theism over naturalism*. No! Even if we supposed that we had reliable evidence about near-death experiences and out-of-body experiences, that evidence could not support the claim that our souls can exist in independence from – or in the absence of – our brains, because, of course, our brains *continue to exist* if we are making reports of these kinds of experiences. And the remaining 'evidence' – alleged communication with the dead, etc. – is evidently susceptible of plausible naturalistic* explaining away (cf. our earlier discussion of reports of miracles and anomalous phenomena).

There are, of course, views about how subjective conscious experiences are related to brain states that have not been considered in the preceding discussion. We have considered only the hypothesis that our subjective conscious experiences are neuro-chemical states and processes, and the hypothesis that our subjective conscious experiences occur in our non-physical souls and interact causally with neuro-chemical states and processes in our brains. However, the hypothesis, that our subjective conscious experiences occur in our non-physical souls and interact causally with neuro-chemical states and processes in our brains, is clearly the *best* case for those who think that our subjective conscious experience favours theism over naturalism: given that even interactive substance

DOI: 10.1057/9781137354143

dualism does not favour theism over naturalism*, we are clearly justified in concluding that our subjective conscious experience does not favour theism over naturalism*. Consequently, we are left in the following position: unless interactive substance dualism is the view about the relation of subjective conscious experience to brain states that is most favoured by the evidence, we should suppose that considerations about subjective conscious experience do not favour theism over naturalism; but, if interactive substance dualism is the view about the relation of subjective conscious experience to brain states that is most favoured by the evidence, we should suppose only that theism is not favoured over naturalism*. Of course, if we think that naturalism* is a kind of naturalism – and that is certainly left open by the account of naturalism that we gave in Chapter 1 – then we don't need to make any qualifications here. In order to simplify future discussion, I shall assume that naturalism* is a kind of naturalism; if this isn't right, then it will be perfectly clear how to rewrite what I say in terms of naturalism* (and naturalism* will become the hypothesis of interest).

Reason and inference

Human beings are capable of engaging in reflective logical and mathematical reasoning; human beings can make inferences involving explicit appeal to logical principles. Moreover, the capacity that human beings have to engage in this kind of reasoning and inference provides them with a systematically reliable way of understanding the world. But, Theist might say, there is no way that Naturalist can account for this capacity: Naturalist must appeal to evolutionary theory in order to explain how this capacity can arise in circumstances in which it is not already present, and yet it is clear that no mere evolutionary explanation of the origination of this capacity can succeed.

Naturalist should agree with Theist that, if it were true that *all* human reasoning and inference is marked with explicit appeal to governing principles, and keyed to the provision of systematically reliable ways of understanding the world, then it is quite implausible to suppose that one could give a merely evolutionary explanation of the human capacity to engage in reasoning and inference. But, in fact, recent developments in cognitive psychology yield overwhelming evidence that much characteristically human reasoning and inference is not marked by explicit appeal to governing principles, and is not keyed to the provision of

DOI: 10.1057/9781137354143

systematically reliable ways of understanding the world. (And, besides, as we noted in earlier discussion, Lewis Carroll's story about Achilles and the Tortoise already tells us that we must engage in reasoning and inference that is not marked by explicit appeal to governing principles if we are to engage in reasoning and inference at all.)

A vast amount of data supports the view that our minds are well-modelled as having two distinct cognitive sub-systems. System 1 is fast, automatic, frugal (i.e. undemanding of cognitive capacity), acquired by biology (together with exposure and experience), heuristic and probably largely modular. System 2 is slow, controlled, expensive (i.e. demanding of cognitive capacity), acquired by enculturation and formal tuition, and located in central processing. Because System 2 is expensive, it is not always available: even though training and formal tuition can extend your capacity to draw on System 2, everyone relies upon System 1 when sufficiently tired or sufficiently emotional, or when System 2 is exhausted through extended use, or when there are no cues or prompts that call System 2 into operation. Moreover, although System 1 is fast and heuristic, System 1 does embed a range of basic logical and mathematical principles: simple Boolean operations and the like.

The outlines of the evolutionary story that goes along with this view of human cognitive psychology are clear. The modules in System 1 are directly selected for, and their fast, automatic and frugal heuristics are keyed to evolutionary success. Of course – as we noted previously – there is a certain amount of logic and reason that is required for evolutionary success: so a certain amount of logic and reason is built into System 1. But it is also the case that System 1's fast, automatic and frugal heuristics lead to all kinds of inferential errors that have been demonstrated and recorded in countless psychological experiments.

System 2 is also directly selected for, as a central processing system: the evolutionary development of central processing correlated with increase in complexity of human social organisation, the development of language and the competitive advantage accrued by human beings who were better predictors of the behaviour of other human beings. However, the capacity to engage in reflective logical and mathematical reasoning – to make inferences involving explicit appeal to logical and mathematical principles as part of a systematically reliable way of understanding the world – is a culturally and educationally moderated by-product, of the development of that central processing system, that builds upon the correct logic and reasoning that is built into System 1.

DOI: 10.1057/9781137354143

When we seek to assess the relative merits of Naturalism and Theism against the data concerning human reason, we need to make sure that we take *all* of the relevant data about human reason into account. We should not focus solely on what is clearly a very special case – our ability to make inferences involving explicit appeal to logical and mathematical principles as part of a systematically reliable way of understanding the world – while paying no attention to all of the rest of our cognitive capacities and abilities. But, when we consider all of the data about human cognitive capacities – and, in particular, when we consider the fast and frugal heuristics that we all use much of the time in our reasoning and inference – it becomes very unclear that the data about human reasoning and inference does support Theism over Naturalism, and, indeed, it might well be that the more inclusive pool of data about human reasoning and inference actually supports Naturalism over Theism. (Certainly, on Standard Theism, it seems rather puzzling why God would make beings with a System 1: why wouldn't a perfectly good, omnipotent, omniscient God have made beings that only had a System 2?)

Taking all of the relevant data about human cognitive capacities into account, it seems that considerations, about our ability to make inferences involving explicit appeal to logical and mathematical principles as part of a systematically reliable way of understanding the world, do not support Theism over Naturalism. On the one hand, the Naturalist can tell a consistent – and, indeed, plausible – story about how human beings acquired the ability to make inferences involving explicit appeal to logical and mathematical principles as part of a systematically reliable way of understanding the world. And, on the other hand, further data about the fast and frugal heuristics that are characteristic of human inference and reason might well be thought to fit better with Naturalism than with Theism. On balance, it seems clearly correct to say that considerations about reason and inference do not favour Theism over Naturalism; and it may even be correct to say that considerations about reason and inference favour Naturalism over Theism.

Religious experience

The eighth piece of evidence that we shall consider is the reported religious experiences of human beings: reports of (1) manifestations of religion – religious practice, religious tradition, religious organisation,

DOI: 10.1057/9781137354143

religious belief and so forth; (2) the world's being 'seen' in religious terms – for example, people's 'seeing' God's handiwork in nature; (3) collective witnessing of miracles; (4) dreams and visions with religious content; and (5) 'mystical' – 'spiritual', 'sacred' – experiences. We shall focus here on the last of these categories, as it is the only one that we do not discuss elsewhere.

There are different kinds of reported 'mystical' experiences. For instance, there are reports of (a) *possession* by the divine (ecstasy, enthusiasm, etc.); (b) *encounter* with the divine (characterised by Rudolf Otto (1869–1937), in his classic *The Idea of the Holy*, in terms of fear, compulsion and a sense of personality); and (c) *sense of oneness* with the divine or nature (characterised by William James (1842–1910), in his classic *The Varieties of Religious Experience*, in terms of evanescence, ineffability, pedagogical value and passivity).

Assessment of the evidential value of 'mystical' experience is not straightforward. On the one hand, 'ecstatic', 'numinous' and 'unitive' experiences are part of the common heritage of humanity; on the other hand, the subjective interpretation of these experiences is highly sensitive to place, culture and a wide range of individual factors.

Suppose that Theist claims that his 'ecstatic', 'numinous' and 'unitive' experiences are direct experiences of God. Should Naturalist acknowledge that Theist's experiences do favour Theism over Naturalism? Should Naturalist admit that it would be mere arrogance on his part to suppose that he knows better than Theist what the evidential implications of Theist's 'mystical' experiences are?

There are many conditions that predispose towards 'mystical' experience: *mental illness* – depression, schizophrenia, epilepsy, stroke; *ingestion of 'mind-altering' drugs* – mescalin, psilocybin; *bodily insult* – starvation, mortification, extreme exercise, extreme sexual activity, near-death experience; *'rhythmical' activities* – meditation, prayer, trance, music, dance, chant; and so forth. These conditions are not noted for their cognitive reliability in other domains: mental illness, ingestion of 'mind-altering' drugs, bodily insult and 'rhythmical' activity are not positively correlated with performance on standard reasoning and inference tasks. Indeed, mental illness, ingestion of 'mind-altering' drugs and bodily insult are all very strongly *negatively* correlated with performance on standard reasoning and inference tasks. If Theist's 'mystical' experiences are caused in these ways, then Naturalist is surely right to question their evidential value.

DOI: 10.1057/9781137354143

But suppose that Theist's 'ecstatic', 'numinous' and 'unitive' experiences are not the results of mental illness, ingestion of 'mind-altering' drugs, bodily insult or 'rhythmical' activities. Suppose, instead, that Theist's 'mystical' experiences are of the Jamesian kind: 'passive' and unprepared. Should Naturalist then admit that it would be mere arrogance on his part to suppose that he knows better than Theist what the evidential implications of Theist's 'mystical' experiences are?

Before we can respond directly to this question, we need to ask whether Naturalist has the kinds of 'mystical' experiences that are now at issue. Does Naturalist have sensations of 'oneness' with the universe – states in which he feels completely at home in the Cosmos? Does Naturalist have 'epiphanies' – intense sensations of looking at familiar things from new perspectives? If Naturalist does have the kinds of 'mystical' experiences that Theist has, but does not interpret these experiences in religious terms, then there is no question of arrogance: the disagreement between Theist and Naturalist in the interpretation of these experiences is perfectly symmetrical. Moreover, given the range of hard-to-interpret experiences – shivers down the spine, variations in mood and affect, feelings of being watched, etc. – that we all experience but do not take as evidence for the existence of a transcendent reality, there is considerable pressure to seek a unified explanation of the full body of this kind of experience in terms of cognitive science and evolutionary theory. (A considerable body of recent psychological research supports the idea that System 1 is strongly prone to over-attribution of agency: we are all disposed to suppose that we have detected agency when in fact there is none. (Think about those noises you sometimes hear when you are lying awake late at night. Surely that's not an intruder in your kitchen!) One way that this may happen is as a result of inference from the evidence of internal states that are appropriately triggered by agents, but which are themselves inclined to over-production. Perhaps this is how personality gets into Otto's account of the 'numinous': over-produced 'fear and trembling, attraction, fascination and compulsion' receives a personal interpretation that, in the absence of any natural candidates, becomes directed towards the transcendent.)

Suppose, finally, that Naturalist simply does not have 'mystical' experiences: there is a range of typically human experiences that Theist has, but Naturalist does not. Might it be that Naturalist is in the position of a blind man disputing the judgments that sighted people make on the basis of what they can see? The analogy is clearly flawed. The blind do

DOI: 10.1057/9781137354143

not dispute the judgments made by sighted people on the basis of what they can see. Why not? Because the blind can test the reliability of those judgments using their other senses: they can acquire *independent* evidence that the vision of sighted people is veridical. But, to the extent that there is a way of testing the reliability of 'mystical' experience as a guide to an independent reality, the result of that evaluation is negative: for, as we noted earlier, there is enormous cultural and individual variation in the interpretation of mystical experiences. Each of the major religions of the world takes 'mystical' experience to be confirmation of its truth, and yet the teachings of the major religions of the world contradict one another. Given the evidence of cross-cultural comparison, it seems more reasonable to suppose that 'mystical' experiences should not be thought of on analogy with the products of our sensory modalities: 'mystical' experiences are not 'connections' with some part or aspect of reality.

When we think about 'mystical' experience in the context of everything that we know about human experience and cognition, we find no reason to suppose that 'mystical' experience favours Theism over Naturalism. However, before we can draw the same conclusion for religious experience more generally – that is, before we can conclude that, when we think about religious experience in the context of everything that we know about human experience and cognition, we find no reason to suppose that religious experience favours Theism over Naturalism – we need to give some further consideration to the evidential value of religion itself.

Scripture, authority, organisation and tradition

The ninth piece of evidence that we shall consider is the scriptures, teachers, organisations and traditions of the world's religions. Writings from the religions of the world that at least some consider holy include the *Vedas*, the *Upanishads* and the *Bhagavad-Gita*; the *Qur'an*, *Hadith* and *Sunnah*; the *Tanakh* and *Talmud*; the *Kojiki*; the *Tao Te Ching*; the *Avesta*; the *Bible*; the *Pali Canon*; the *Four Books* and the *Five Classics*; the *Satkhandagama*; the *Epistles of Wisdom*; and so forth. Figures from the religions of the world that at least some consider holy include Mohammed, Buddha, Confucius, Zoroaster, Moses, Krishna, Jesus, Lao-Tzu, Imhotep and many others. The religions of the world have distinct clerical hierarchies, holy places, rituals, festivals, feasts, music, meditative practices

DOI: 10.1057/9781137354143

and so forth. Consider, for example, the range of holy days: Ridvan, Holi, Diwali, Ramadan, Al-Hijira, Shogatsu, Shubun-sai, Wesak, Asala, Samhain, Yule, Vaisakhi, Hola Mohalla, Christmas, Easter, Hannukah, Yom Kippur, Khordad Sal, Jamshedi Noruz and so on.

The doctrines of some of the religions of the world entail Theism; the doctrines of other of the religions of the world are consistent with Theism; and the doctrines of the remaining religions of the world are inconsistent with Theism. Given the inconsistency in the teachings of the world religions, it seems that the *content* of the teachings of world religions favours neither Theism nor Naturalism. In order to argue from the doctrines of some subset of the religions of the world to Theism, one would need some independent reason for supposing that the doctrines of that subset of the religions of the world are *true* (while the doctrines of the remaining religions of the world are not true). But, if there is some independent reason for supposing that the doctrines of that subset of the religions of the world are true, then we don't need to appeal to the contents of those doctrines in order to reach the conclusion that Theism is to be preferred to Naturalism.

It also seems that the facts about the diversity of the scriptures, teachers, organisations and traditions of the religions of the world favour neither Naturalism nor Theism. On the one hand (Minimal) Theism entails nothing about the beliefs, desires and intentions of God, beyond whatever is entailed by God's being the cause of the existence of the natural world, and the source or ground or origin of most – if not all – of its significant features. Consequently, one might think that (Minimal) Theism fits equally well with diversity of scriptures, teachings, organisations and traditions in the religions of the world and with uniformity in the scriptures, teachings, organisations and traditions of the religions of the world. On the other hand (Minimal) Naturalism also fits equally well with diversity of scriptures, teachings, organisations and traditions in the religions of the world and with uniformity in the scriptures, teachings, organisations and traditions of the religions of the world. Perhaps recent developments in the cognitive science of religion might have been used to predict diversity of scriptures, teachings, organisations and traditions in the religions of the world; but those developments in the cognitive science of religion – discussed in the preceding sections – can be accommodated equally well by (Minimal) Theism and (Minimal) Naturalism.

It may well be that considerations about scripture, authorities, teachers, organisations, traditions and so forth loom very large in the *explanation*

DOI: 10.1057/9781137354143

of the distribution of religious belief. No one will be surprised to learn that most people share the religious beliefs of their parents, families and immediate communities. However, it is surely to be expected that these same considerations about scripture, authorities, teachers, organisations and traditions carry no significant *justificatory* role for religious belief. When we ask whether we should prefer Theism to Naturalism (or vice versa), we cannot reasonably expect that considerations about scriptures, authorities, teachers, organisations, traditions (and religious experiences) will favour Theism over Naturalism. This point is reflected in the further fact that it is acknowledged on almost all hands that arguments from scripture, authority, tradition and experience are very weak arguments for the existence of God. If the existence of God cannot be argued on other grounds, then it is a forlorn hope to suppose that it might be argued on grounds of scripture, authority, tradition and religious experience.

Concluding remarks

We have considered the bearing of a wide range of evidence on (Minimal) Theism and (Minimal) Naturalism: the concept of God, global causal structure, cosmic fine-tuning, history of the earth, history of humanity, a priori knowledge, morality and human flourishing, consciousness and reason, religious experience, and scripture, authority, organisation and tradition. We began by observing that, apart from the consideration of evidence (Minimal) Naturalism has an advantage over (Minimal Theism), namely, that it is simpler: it postulates fewer and less complex primitive entities; it has fewer and less complex primitive features; it appeals to fewer and less complex primitive principles. We then noted that none of the evidence that we considered favoured (Minimal) Theism over (Minimal) Naturalism. The conclusion that we should draw is that, at least given the evidence that we have examined to this point, (Minimal) Naturalism is to be preferred to (Minimal) Theism.

Of course, this is not a very strong conclusion. For one thing, there may be other evidence that we have not considered that would tilt the balance in favour of (Minimal) Theism. (Against this, though, it should be borne in mind that we have surveyed the evidence that bears on all of the historically important arguments for the existence of God. If there is further evidence that would tilt the balance in favour of (Minimal) Theism, it would be evidence that has not hitherto been thought to be

DOI: 10.1057/9781137354143

significant.) For another thing, there are many details in the assessment that we have carried out that could be contested. Our main aim has to be to introduce the kinds of considerations that ought to be taken into account in a judicious weighing of the merits of Theism and Naturalism; we shall return later to the question whether we can reasonably expect to secure agreement about the outcome of such judicious weighing.

References and further reading

On ontological arguments: Graham Oppy (1996) *Ontological Arguments and Belief in God* Cambridge: Cambridge University Press; Graham Oppy (2006) *Arguing about Gods* Cambridge: Cambridge University Press; Kevin Harrelson (2009) *The Ontological Argument from Descartes to Hegel* Amherst: Prometheus Books.
On cosmological arguments: William Rowe (1975) *The Cosmological Argument* Princeton: Princeton University Press; William Lane Craig (1979) *The Cosmological Argument from Plato to Leibniz* London: Macmillan; Alexander Pruss (2006) *The Principle of Sufficient Reason: A Reassessment* Cambridge: Cambridge University Press.
On teleological arguments: Neil Manson (ed.) (2003) *God and Design: The Teleological Argument and Modern Science* London: Routledge. On cosmic fine-tuning arguments: John Leslie (1989) *Universes* London: Routledge; Roger White (2000) 'Fine-Tuning and Multiple Universes' *Noûs* 34, 260–76. On biological arguments: William Paley (2006) *Natural Theology*, Matthew Eddy and David Knight (eds) Oxford: Oxford University Press; William Dembski and Michael Ruse (eds) (2004) *Debating Design: From Darwin to DNA* Cambridge: Cambridge University Press.
On miracles: Richard Swinburne (ed.) (1989) *Miracles* New York: Macmillan; John Earman (2000) *Hume's Abject Failure: The Argument against Miracles* Oxford: Oxford University Press; Alan Hájek (2008) 'Are Miracles Chimerical?' *Oxford Studies in Philosophy of Religion* 1, 82–104.
On morality and human flourishing: Gregory Paul (2005) 'Cross-National Correlations of Quantifiable Societal Health with Popular Religiosity and Secularism in the Prosperous Democracies' *Journal of Religion and Society* 7, 1–17; Phil Zuckermann (2008) *Society without*

DOI: 10.1057/9781137354143

God: What the Least Religious Nations Can Tell Us about Contentment
New York: New York University Press.

On consciousness and reason: Robert Adams (1987) 'Flavors, Colors, and God' in his *The Virtue of Faith and other Essays in Philosophical Theology* Oxford: Oxford University Press, 243–62; Victor Reppert (2003) *C. S. Lewis' Dangerous Idea: In Defense of the Argument from Reason* Downer's Grove, IL: InterVarsity Press. For zombies: David Chalmers (1996) *The Conscious Mind* Oxford: Oxford University Press. For System 1 and System 2: Daniel Kahnemann (2011) *Thinking, Fast and Slow* London: Penguin.

On religious experience: Rudolf Otto (1958) *The Idea of the Holy*, second edition Oxford: Oxford University Press; William James (1960) *The Varieties of Religious Experience* London: Collins. Jeffrey Schloss and Michael Murray (eds) (2009) *The Believing Primate: Scientific, Philosophical and Theological Reflections on the Origins of Religion* Oxford: Oxford University Press.

DOI: 10.1057/9781137354143

4
Standard Theism and Naturalism

Abstract: *We compare expanded versions of our theories – Standard Theism and Standard Naturalism – on a further range of data. We begin by noting that Standard Theism is trumped by Standard Naturalism on the data considered in the previous chapter. We then consider, in turn: horrendous suffering, salvation, meaning and purpose, and hiddenness and non-belief. We argue that none of the new data that we introduce favours theism over naturalism. We conclude that, given all of the data considered, naturalism trumps theism.*

Keywords: Epicurus; evil; hiddenness; meaning; non-belief; Pascal's Wager; purpose; salvation; suffering

Oppy, Graham. *The Best Argument against God.* Basingstoke: Palgrave Macmillan, 2013. DOI: 10.1057/9781137354143.

We are now going to compare the theoretical virtues of Standard Theism and Naturalism in connection with a range of considerations ('data'). Recall that, according to Standard Theism, God is the omnipotent, omniscient and omnibenevolent source, or ground or originating cause of everything that can have a source, or ground or originating cause.

Given that Standard Theism involves a (slightly) more developed conception of God than is afforded by Minimal Theism, there might be reason to reconsider all of the data that was appealed to in the previous chapter in our assessment of the comparative merits of Minimal Theism and Naturalism. However, we shall leave it to you to consider whether the move to Standard Theism makes any difference to the assessment of the comparative merits of Theism and Naturalism on all of that already discussed data. (My own view – which I shall take for granted in what follows – is that the move makes no difference: the evidence considered to this point favours Standard Naturalism over Standard Theism.)

Horrendous suffering

You are about to enter a country that you have never entered before. You are told that the country is ruled by a very powerful, very wise and very good – benevolent, merciful, just, etc. – sovereign who is fully in control of the country. Moreover, you are told that the country is more than amply resourced, and not subject to external threats: it is not at war, subject to famine, devastated by natural disasters or the like.

When you first view the country, as you approach the border from the surrounding hills, you are struck by the richness of its agriculture, the abundance of its water supply, the magnificence of its cities and so forth. From this initial vantage point, it seems pretty clear that it is true that the country is both amply resourced, and not subject to external threats.

However, when you cross the border and enter the country, you discover – to your horror – that there are grotesquely violated corpses hanging from lamp-posts along the road that you travel, including corpses of babies and young children. In the light of this discovery, it seems that you have reason to reassess the information that you were initially given. If it is so that the country is amply resourced and not subject to external threats, then surely it is not the case that the country is fully under the control of a very powerful, very wise and very good – benevolent, merciful, just, etc. – sovereign. A very good sovereign who

DOI: 10.1057/9781137354143

was in full control of the country would not authorise, or even permit, the murder of babies, young children, or, indeed, of any of the citizens of the country. Given your evidence, the plausible view to form is that either the sovereign is powerless to prevent the murder of babies and young children, or the sovereign is somehow ignorant of the murder of babies and young children, or the sovereign is much less than morally virtuous (indifferent to suffering, lacking mercy, malicious or the like).

(Standard) Theism says that there is an omnipotent, omniscient and perfectly good God who is the cause of the existence of the natural world, and the source or ground or origin of most – if not all – of its significant features. But our world is undeniably filled with horrendous suffering: think, for example about horrendous human and animal suffering that has primarily *natural* causes – earthquakes, tsunamis, hurricanes, tornados, floods, droughts, bushfires, crop failures, plagues, epidemics and so on; and also think about horrendous human (and sometimes animal) suffering that is consequent upon the actions of (human) *moral* agents – genocide, mass murder, war, torture, pack rape and so forth. So – in line with our story about the allegedly wise, powerful and good sovereign – shouldn't we conclude that we have reason to doubt the claim that there is an omnipotent, omniscient and perfectly good God who is the cause of the existence of the natural world, and the source or ground or origin of most – if not all – of its significant features? More strongly – and more importantly for our present purposes – shouldn't we conclude that evidence about horrendous suffering is evidence that *favours* Standard Naturalism over Standard Theism? After all, there is no reason to suppose that the evidence about horrendous suffering is in tension with Standard Naturalism, and perhaps there is even some reason to think that the evidence about horrendous suffering is to be expected if Standard Naturalism is true.

There are various ways in which one might try to argue that there is no tension between the evidence of horrendous suffering and Standard Theism.

Perhaps, for example, one might try to argue that there is no such thing as suffering: really, there is merely the absence of non-suffering (or flourishing). But this playing with words seems hopeless. After all, why shouldn't we think that horrendous absence of non-flourishing is in tension with Standard Theism, but not in tension with Standard Naturalism? The horror of the Holocaust is not diminished by calling it 'absence of non-suffering'.

DOI: 10.1057/9781137354143

Perhaps one might try to argue that suffering is required for appreciation of freedom from suffering: if there were no suffering, then there would be no appreciation of the good things in our world. Against this, it might be objected that an omnipotent and omniscient being could surely have created us with a vivid innate appreciation of the good things in our world that was not dependent upon any actual experiences of suffering. But, even if that isn't right, the obvious difficulty with the argument is that so much of the horrendous suffering that is found in our world is surplus to the alleged requirement: we could vividly appreciate the good things in our world without suffering anywhere near as much as we do. Moreover, there are instances of horrendous suffering that simply cannot be justified in these terms: for instance, very young babies that are raped and killed do not develop any appreciation of the good things in our world because they do not live long enough for the relevant appreciative capacities to develop.

Perhaps one might try to argue that creatures can have lives of genuine value only if there are ways in which they suffer, or, at the very least, ways in which they are vulnerable to suffering: suffering or vulnerability to suffering is necessary for worthwhile human development. But this suggestion is subject to the same difficulties as the previous proposal. Surely we could have lives of genuine value in the absence of much of the horrendous suffering that is to be found in our world. And, in any case, much of the horrendous suffering that is to be found in the world prevents development of appreciation of the good things in our world.

Perhaps one might try to argue that the horrendous suffering that is to be found in our world is justified in terms of the good of freedom: it is better that the world contain unconstrained free agents who cause the kinds of horrendous suffering that are to be found in our world than that the world contain somewhat constrained agents who, while free to bring about a certain amount of suffering, are unable to cause the kinds of horrendous suffering that are to be found in our world. Against this, it might be said: surely unconstrained freedom can't be worth that much! If the world were just as it is, except that there was an additional module in the human brain that ensured that no one would willingly rape and kill babies, is it really true that the world would be a worse place? And, in any case, the putative great goodness of unconstrained freedom affords no explanation at all of horrendous suffering that has primarily natural causes: earthquakes, tsunamis, hurricanes, tornados, floods, droughts, bushfires, crop failures, plagues, epidemics and so on.

DOI: 10.1057/9781137354143

Perhaps one might try to argue that, the claim at the end of the preceding paragraph notwithstanding, the putative great goodness of unconstrained freedom does explain all of the horrendous suffering that appears to have primarily natural causes, because all of these things that appear to have primarily natural causes – earthquakes, tsunamis, hurricanes, tornados, floods, droughts, bushfires, crop failures, plagues, epidemics and so on – are actually the work of other supernatural agents: demons, devils, angels and the like. However, in the context of a debate about the relative merits of Naturalism and Theism, this is not a winning move: for the postulation of demons, devils, angels and so forth further increases the advantage that Naturalism enjoys over Theism in terms of simplicity, and yet cannot do more than merely neutralise the implications of horrendous suffering.

Perhaps one might try to argue that the claim, that the evidence about horrendous suffering is in tension with Standard Theism, overlooks implications of God's omnipotence and omniscience. True enough, it might be said, violated corpses of babies and young children hanging from lamp-posts would be evidence against the claim that a country is fully under the control of a very powerful, very wise and very good – benevolent, merciful, just, etc. – human sovereign. But it doesn't follow from this that the horrendous suffering that is to be found in our world is evidence against the claim that our world is fully under the control of an omnipotent, omniscient and perfectly good source, or ground, or originating cause of everything that can have a source, or ground, or originating cause. For, while we can be fairly confident that we have what it takes to understand the actions of a very powerful, very wise and very good – benevolent, merciful, just, etc. – human sovereign, it is surely not the case that we can be confident at all that we have what it takes to understand the actions of an omnipotent, omniscient and perfectly good source, or ground, or originating cause of everything that can have a source, or ground, or originating cause. Who are we to say what considerations an omnipotent and omniscient being takes into account? Who are we to deny that there might be goods that we cannot know about that justify the horrendous suffering that is to be found in our world?

If the horrendous suffering of an individual is to be justified, then surely it must be justified in terms of benefits to the individual who undergoes the horrific suffering in question: if the horrendous suffering of a young baby that is raped and killed is justified, then it is justified in terms of benefits that accrue to the baby in question. But, if this is right, then there is a straightforward argument that there are no goods that

DOI: 10.1057/9781137354143

we cannot know about that accrue to this baby: after all, the existence of the baby is brought to an end by the very horrendous suffering whose justification is in question. We do not need to deny that there might be goods of which an omnipotent and omniscient being has cognisance but of which we cannot have cognisance. We do not need to suppose that we have what it takes to understand all of the actions of an omnipotent, omniscient and perfectly good being. All we need to note is that it would be *obscene* to suppose that the baby obtains some great goods while it is being raped and killed, and it would be *absurd* to suppose that the baby obtains some great goods after it ceases to exist.

Perhaps one might try to argue that the horrendous suffering that is to be found in our world is justified in terms of benefits that are to be experienced in the life to come. (Perhaps, for example, there are great *heavenly* goods of which we can have no cognisance that will come to the baby that is raped and killed.) However, this suggestion invites the same response as the proposal that horrendous suffering that appears to have primarily natural causes is the work of other supernatural agents: this suggestion further increases the advantage that Naturalism has over Theism in terms of simplicity, and yet can do no more than merely neutralise the implications of horrendous suffering. (Of course, there are other difficulties that face the suggestion that there is a life to come. But we shall not take up consideration of those difficulties here.)

Perhaps unsurprisingly, the conclusion that we reach is that considerations about horrendous evil pretty clearly favour (Standard) Naturalism over (Standard) Theism. While there may be ways in which Theism can be rendered consistent with the amounts and kinds of horrendous evil that are to be found in our world, the price of any such rendering would be to further increase the advantage that Naturalism has over Theism in terms of simplicity. Adding considerations about horrendous evil to considerations about the concept of God, global causal structure, cosmic fine-tuning, history of the earth, history of humanity, a priori knowledge, morality and human flourishing, consciousness and reason, religious experience, scripture, authority, organisation and tradition does not defeat the reason that we previously had to prefer Naturalism to Theism.

Epicurus on evil

Some people have thought that considerations about evil decisively defeat (Standard) Theism. So, for example, Epicurus (341–270 BCE) – and

DOI: 10.1057/9781137354143

countless people after him – have supposed that the mere existence of evil is simply inconsistent with the existence of God:

> Is God willing to prevent evil, but not able? Then is he impotent. Is God able, but not willing? Then is he malevolent. Is he both able and willing? Whence then is evil? (D. Hume, *Dialogues Concerning Natural Religion*, edited by H. D. Aiken, New York: Hafner Press, 1948, 66)

Suppose that we agree that, amongst universes in which there are free moral agents, the best universes are all among those universes in which the agents in question always freely choose the good. Suppose that we agree, further, that the best universes are all among universes in which there are free moral agents. Then, if God could just choose to make a universe in which there are free moral agents who always freely choose the good, then that is the choice that God would make. As our universe is not one in which free moral agents always freely choose the good – after all, whether or not they are free moral agents, human beings do not always choose the good – it follows that, if our universe was made by God, then God can't just choose to make a universe in which there are free moral agents. Why might this be?

Suppose, first, that we adopt a libertarian conception of freedom. On this conception of freedom, agents act freely just in case they could have done any of a range of things in the very circumstances in which they acted. But suppose that the very circumstances in which an agent acts are circumstances that God has brought about (in part) because that agent will perform a particular good action in those circumstances. If God has brought about circumstances (in part) because a given agent will perform a particular good action in those circumstances, then it is impossible for that agent to do anything else in those circumstances. Given that God is omnipotent and omniscient, it is impossible that both (i) God brings about circumstances (in part) because a given agent will perform a particular good action in those circumstances and (ii) that agent does not perform the action in question in the circumstances in question. But then, on the libertarian conception of freedom, the agent does not act freely in the circumstances in question. So, on the libertarian conception of freedom, God cannot just choose to make a universe in which there are free agents who all always freely choose the good.

Suppose, second, that we adopt a compatibilist conception of freedom. On this conception of freedom, agents act freely just in case they act on their normally acquired mental states – beliefs, desires, intentions and so

DOI: 10.1057/9781137354143

forth – in the absence of a range of defeating conditions. In particular, one of the potential defeating conditions for a given agent is that there is another agent who has direct control over the mental states of the first agent: if the second agent chooses or selects the mental states of the first agent, then that undermines the freedom of the first agent. But, if God brings about circumstances (in part) because a given agent will perform a particular action on the basis of given mental states in those circumstances, then the agent will not have compatibilist freedom in those circumstances, as the agent's belief, desires, intentions and so forth will ultimately have been chosen or selected by God. So, again, on the compatibilist conception of freedom, God cannot just choose to make a universe in which there are free agents who all always freely choose the good.

Whichever conception of freedom we adopt, it turns out that we are required to deny that God can just choose to make a universe in which there are free agents who all always freely choose the good. But then, if we agree that God would do best to make a universe in which there are free agents, it follows that God can make a universe containing free agents only if the actions of those free agents are not determined by God's universe-making activities. In the terminology introduced earlier in this book, God will have to make agents whose actions are chancy. And then, as it is logically impossible that the chancy agents of actions are determined in advance, it is no threat to God's omnipotence that he is unable to determine the actions of the agents that he makes. Of course, if God is lucky, the free agents he makes will turn out to all always freely choose the good – but it is to be expected that this will not be the case.

Of course, this reply to Epicurus depends upon the substantive assumption that freedom is so valuable that the best universes will be among the universes in which there are free agents. If that assumption is denied, then it seems plausible – to me, anyway – that God would make a universe in which no agents ever caused other agents to suffer. Perhaps it might be objected that it is unclear what reason God would have to create a universe in which there are no free agents: why bother to make agents whose actions are antecedently determined? But, it might be responded, this is just an instance of a more general worry: for, given that God knows all possibilities in advance, what reason would God have to create any universe at all? What is the value – to God – of realising one possibility amongst the array of possibilities of which God already has complete knowledge?

DOI: 10.1057/9781137354143

Be all this as it may, it seems to me that we have more than enough reason to suppose that Epicurus' argument does not provide a knock-down objection to Theism: there are various ways in which the mere existence of evil might be reconciled with the existence of an omnipotent, omniscient, perfectly good source, or ground, or originating cause of everything that can have a source, or ground, or originating cause.

Salvation

Different religions have different views about the goal of life, and the methods by which the goal is achieved. For some religions, the goal is escape from suffering – and, in particular, escape from an unending cycle of death and rebirth – either through annihilation, or through absorption into some greater whole (a world spirit, or the like). For other religions, the goal is to go to the best destination in the life to come – in particular, to go to Heaven, to dwell in eternity with God, and not to go to Hell, to suffer excruciating torment for eternity. These diverse beliefs about the goal of life connect to diverse metaphysical beliefs about the global structure of reality, the nature of persons and personal identity, and about the methods by which the goal is to be achieved: keeping the law, living a life of inward devotion, performing purification rites, observing the five pillars, following the noble eight-fold path, taking up one of the yogas (bhakti, karma, rāja or jñaña), undergoing baptism (and perhaps hoping for the bestowal of divine grace) and so forth.

Might the differing responses that Naturalism and Theism make to this range of beliefs about salvation yield a reason for preferring one to the other? On the one hand, Naturalism rejects all religious views about the goal of life, and the methods by which the goal is achieved. According to Naturalism, there is no esoteric or occult goal to life: no unending cycle of death and rebirth, no Heaven, no Hell and so forth. Thus, Naturalism denies that there is any prospect of – or any need for – achieving any kind of salvation. On the other hand, Theism is frequently coupled with further claims about esoteric or occult goals for life: in particular, claims about other domains – Heaven and Hell – that are directly ruled by God, and in which rewards and punishments are distributed according to behaviour in the present life. According to most who espouse some kind of Theism, there is reason to hope for better in the world that is to

DOI: 10.1057/9781137354143

come ... and the underwriting or permission of this hope is a significant advantage that Theism enjoys over Naturalism.

The central issue here isn't really about *hope*. After all, it doesn't seem that there is anything inconsistent in one's holding certain beliefs, and yet hoping that the beliefs that one holds are false. Even if all the evidence seems to point one way, you can still reasonably *hope* that the evidence you have is misleading. So it cannot be that Theism enjoys a significant advantage over Naturalism because it underwrites or permits *hope* that there is a better world to come.

The central issue is about *belief*. What Naturalism has that Theism does not have is a commitment to the non-existence of Heaven and Hell: according to Naturalism, there is no supernatural post-mortem realm in which we coexist with God, the Devil, angels, demons and whatever other supernatural agents are supposed to populate that realm. Of course, there is nothing in Standard Theism that *entails* that there is a supernatural post-mortem realm in which we coexist with God, the Devil, angels, demons and whatever other supernatural agents are supposed to populate that realm: but many (if not most) theists do believe that there is a supernatural post-mortem realm in which we coexist with God, the Devil, angels, demons and whatever other supernatural agents are supposed to populate that realm.

Should we suppose that Theism enjoys a significant advantage over Naturalism because it is consistent with the hypothesis that there is a supernatural post-mortem realm in which we coexist with God, the Devil, angels, demons and whatever other supernatural agents are supposed to populate that realm? Well, surely that depends upon whether there is evidence that counts in favour of the claim that there is a supernatural post-mortem realm in which we coexist with God, the Devil, angels, demons and whatever other supernatural agents are supposed to populate that realm! In particular, we can hardly find here a reason to prefer Theism to Naturalism if we also allow that there is no evidence that there is a supernatural post-mortem realm in which we coexist with God, the Devil, angels, demons and whatever other supernatural agents are supposed to populate that realm. But alleged evidence for the existence of such a realm – near-death experiences, out-of-body experiences, séances, reports of communication with the dead and so forth – is prey to the kinds of difficulties that beset reports of miracles (discussed earlier in connection with the 'history of humanity'). Given that there is no other reason to prefer Theism to Naturalism, it would be clutching at

DOI: 10.1057/9781137354143

straws to suppose that the kind of testimonial evidence in question here supports Theism over Naturalism.

Perhaps, though, we have been too quick to insist that the central issue here is about belief rather than hope. Even if we accept that the evidence doesn't count in favour of Theistic belief, might we nonetheless have reason to try to cultivate belief in Theism, on the grounds that, if Theism is true and we believe it, we are in the running to acquire great goods that we can be certain we will not otherwise acquire? William James (1842–1910) and Blaise Pascal (1623–62) are two philosophers who have endorsed this line of thought; in what follows, we shall explore a famous argument developed by Pascal.

Pascal's wager

In his *Pensées*, Blaise Pascal develops an argument for 'wagering for God', that is, for setting out on whatever course of action you judge to be most likely to bring you to a state in which you believe in God. In order to determine whether the prudential considerations to which Pascal adverts might give us a reason to prefer Theism to Naturalism, we begin by listing the premises and conclusion of a modern formulation of Pascal's argument. We leave it to the reader to think about acceptable chains of reasoning that move from the premises to the conclusion.

1   There are two mutually exclusive possible states of the world: either God exists or God does not exist. (Premise)

2   There are two possible courses of action: either you wager for God, or you fail to wager for God. (Premise)

3   The value of wagering for God, if God exists, is infinite; the values of all other combinations, of possible course of action and possible state of affairs, are finite. (Premise)

4   The probability that God exists is non-zero and finite. Call this probability p; then, the probability that God does not exist is $1-p$. (Premise)

5   The expected value of wagering for God = ((the probability that God exists) × (the value of wagering for God if God exists)) + ((the probability that God does not exist) × (the value of wagering for God if God does not exist)) = (p × (infinite value)) + (($1-p$) × (finite value)) = infinite value. (Premise)

6   The expected value of not wagering for God = ((the probability that God exists) × (the value of not wagering for God if God exists)) +

DOI: 10.1057/9781137354143

((the probability that God does not exist) × (the value of not wagering for God if God does not exist)) = (p × (finite value)) + (($1-p$) × (finite value)) = finite value. (Premise)

7 Rationality requires that you always act so as to maximise the expected value of your action. (Premise)

8 (Therefore) You should wager for God. (From 1–7)

There are many objections that can be lodged against this argument. Perhaps the most important objection arises from consideration of what might be called 'mixed strategies'. Consider the following possible course of action: I will defer wagering for God until I win the state lottery for the third consecutive weekend, and then I will wager for God. ('Just a small sign, please!')

If I pursue this course of action, then there are two mutually exclusive possible states of the world: either I win the state lottery on three consecutive weekends and wager for God, or else I don't win the state lottery on three consecutive weekends and don't wager for God.

Call the probability that I win the state lottery on three consecutive weekends r; the probability that I don't win the state lottery on three consecutive weekends is therefore $1-r$. Both values are non-zero and finite.

The value, of winning the state lottery on three weekends and then wagering for God, is the sum of the values of winning the state lottery – finite – and the expected value of wagering for God – infinite. That is, the value of winning the state lottery on three weekends and then wagering for God is infinite. On the other hand, the value, of not winning the state lottery on three weekends and not wagering for God, is the sum of the values of not winning the state lottery – finite – and the expected value of not wagering for God – finite. That is, the value, of not winning the state lottery on three weekends and not wagering for God, is finite.

The expected value of deferring wagering for God until I win the state lottery for the third consecutive weekend and then wagering for God = ((the probability that I win the state lottery on three consecutive weekends) × (the value of winning the state lottery on three consecutive weekends and wagering for God)) + ((the probability that I don't win the state lottery on three consecutive weekends) × (the value of not winning the state lottery on three consecutive weekends and not wagering for God)) = (r × (infinite value) + (($1-r$) × finite value)) = infinite value.

In other words, the expected value of wagering for God is *exactly the same as* the expected value of deferring wagering for God until I win the

DOI: 10.1057/9781137354143

state lottery for the third consecutive weekend (and then wagering for God). Whence, the advice that we should always act so as to maximise the expected value of our actions does *not* tell us to wager for God.

Pascal's argument does not work! Not only that, once we've seen a calculation involving a 'mixed strategy', we see that the difficulty is terminal: if you accept that your decisions should be determined by the aim of maximising expected value, then, in the presence of a source of infinite value, you are simply unable to choose between 'pure strategies' and 'mixed strategies'.

Perhaps you might think that the decision rule needs amendment: if you are calculating in a situation in which all values are finite, and there are only finitely many possible states, then act so as to maximise expected value; but, in the presence of infinite value, simply act in whichever way is most likely to secure the infinite value for you. Even if you are not bothered by the *ad hoc* nature of this proposal, there is an evident difficulty: for surely we must allow that, if we can *conceive* of one way in which infinite value might be available to us, we can *conceive* of many incompatible ways in which infinite value might be available to us. Perhaps, for example, infinite value goes to all and only those who believe that the favourite number of the guardians of infinite value is 17. Or, perhaps, instead, infinite value goes to all and only those who believe that the favourite number of the guardians of infinite value is 29. As I *cannot* set out both to acquire the belief that the favourite number of the guardians of infinite value is 17 and to acquire the belief that the favourite number of the guardians of infinite value is 29 – and because, *ex hypothesi*, I have no more reason to suppose that the favourite number of the guardians of infinite value is 17 that I have reason to suppose that the favourite number of the guardians of infinite value is 29, and *vice versa* – I need more guidance than is given in the suggestion that I act in whatever way is most likely to secure infinite value for me.

In response to the problem of the many conceivable sources of infinite value, it might be said: there is only one *conceivable* source of infinite value that is also a *possible* source of infinite value, namely, God; and an omnipotent, omniscient and perfectly good source, or ground, or originating cause of everything that can have a source, or ground, or originating cause would not – and perhaps even could not – make the attainment of infinite value conditional on correct belief about that being's favourite number. However, even if this is what Theist thinks, there is no reason why Naturalist is required to agree.

DOI: 10.1057/9781137354143

Suppose, for example, that Naturalist does not believe that it is possible that there is a source of infinite value. As it is essential to the calculation that lies at the heart of Pascal's argument that we attribute probabilities to *possible* states of affairs, and values to pairs of actions and *possible* states of affairs, it follows that Pascal's argument could not yield a reason to prefer Theism to Naturalism: if Naturalist does not believe that it is possible that there is a source of infinite value, then the calculation that lies at the heart of the wager argument merely *presupposes* the falsity of Naturalism.

Or, to take another example: observe that, whereas many Christians maintain that infinite value is available only to those who accept Jesus Christ as their Lord and Saviour, many Muslims maintain that infinite value is available only to those who accept that there is no God but Allah and Mohammed is his prophet. It is scarcely to be believed that there are Naturalists who suppose that it is *possible* that infinite value is available only to those who accept Jesus Christ as their Lord and Saviour, but *not possible* that infinite value is available only to those who accept that there is no God but Allah and Mohammed is his prophet, or vice versa. But a Naturalist who supposes that it is *possible* that infinite value is available only to those who accept Jesus Christ as their Lord and Saviour, and also *possible* that infinite value is available only to those who accept that there is no God but Allah and Mohammed is his prophet, can reasonably insist that Pascal's wager provides no help at all in deciding between 'wagering' options. Moreover, a Naturalist may also observe that, whereas many Christians maintain that infinite disvalue accrues to those who fail to accept Jesus Christ as their Lord and Saviour, many Muslims maintain that infinite disvalue accrues to those who fail to accept that there is no God but Allah and Mohammed is his prophet. A Naturalist who supposes that it is possible that infinite disvalue accrues to those who fail to accept Jesus Christ as their Lord and Saviour, and that it is possible that infinite disvalue accrues to those who fail to accept that there is no God but Allah and Mohammed is his prophet, will have even more reason to insist that Pascal's wager is no help at all in the decision between 'wagering' options. (What is 'infinite value' minus 'infinite value'? The most plausible view, I think, is that it is undefined!)

Of course, our discussion to this point has not explored all of the objections that have been made against Pascal's wager. However, this is not the place to try to undertake a more exhaustive investigation. Even without considering other reasons for thinking that Pascal's wager is

DOI: 10.1057/9781137354143

unconvincing, it seems that we are well justified in maintaining that Pascal's wager provides no help at all in the decision between Theism and Naturalism.

Meaning and purpose

A very common complaint about Naturalism is that it entails that our lives have no meaning and no purpose. If it is true both that Naturalism entails that our lives have no meaning and purpose and that Theism does not entail that our lives have no meaning and purpose, then this might be thought to be a consideration that favours Theism over Naturalism.

There are various ways in which the complaint that Naturalism entails that our lives have no meaning and no purpose might be understood.

Perhaps, for example, it might be alleged that the lives of Naturalists are meaningless and purposeless. In order to assess this allegation, let us begin by considering Aristotle's account of the good life. According to Aristotle, a flourishing human being is a flourishing member of a flourishing community (*Politics*, Book VII, esp. xiii). A flourishing person exercises moral and intellectual virtues: a flourishing person has genuine friendships (*Ethics*, Books VIII and IX), exercises both theoretical and practical wisdom (*Ethics*, Book VI) and acts with a range of virtues in pursuit of valuable individual and collective ends (*Ethics*, Books III and IV). And a flourishing human being is not subject to certain kinds of liabilities: a flourishing human being is not impoverished, or unhealthy, or the victim of misfortunes such as bereavements and the like (*Ethics*, Book I, esp. ix–xi). While there is certainly room to quibble with the details of the Aristotelian account, the overall picture that it paints seems – to me, anyway – to be quite attractive.

It is obvious that Naturalists can live the Aristotelian good life: they can live meaningful, purposeful, flourishing human lives. Moreover, it is equally obvious that there is no reason to suppose that Theists are better equipped than Naturalists to live the Aristotelian good life: Naturalists and Theists alike can find meaning and purpose in familial relationships, friendships, exercises of moral and intellectual virtue, engagements in intrinsically rewarding individual and collective pursuits, and so forth. Finally, it is hardly any less obvious that those who cannot find meaning and purpose in familial relationships, friendships, exercises of moral and intellectual virtue, engagements in intrinsically rewarding individual

DOI: 10.1057/9781137354143

and collective pursuits, and so forth, are unlikely to find meaning and purpose anywhere else. Naturalists can – and do – live the Aristotelian good life; to suppose otherwise is just to fall into thoughtless prejudice.

Perhaps it might be alleged that Naturalists are required to suppose that their lives lack meaning and purpose, that is, that Naturalists cannot have available to them a conception of meaning and purpose on which their lives are imbued with meaning and purpose. However, the response that we framed to the previous allegation shows that this allegation is also without substance. Naturalists can accept a broadly Aristotelian account of human flourishing, and they can correctly suppose that their own lives meet this broadly Aristotelian standard. As before, to suppose otherwise is just to fall into unthinking prejudice.

Perhaps it might be alleged that Naturalism entails that our lives have no meaning and no purpose because, if Naturalism is true, then it is very likely that human beings shall eventually vanish from the universe, and leave not a trace. According to current physical theories, from about 10^{130} years into the future, the entire universe will consist of nothing but an enormously dilute gas of the smallest types of elementary particles and very low-energy radiation. (See, for example, the discussion in F. Adams and G. Loughlin *The Five Ages of the Universe* New York: Free Press, 1999.) So, from 10^{130} years on, no traces of human activity will remain in the universe – and, even if there were such traces, there would be no one around to take account of them. But, if we shall eventually have vanished without a trace – if, indeed, from about 10^{130} years into the future, the entire universe will consist of nothing but an enormously dilute gas of the smallest types of elementary particles and very low-energy radiation – doesn't it follow that our existence is meaningless and purposeless?

I don't see why. Certainly, from an Aristotelian perspective, this doesn't follow. The meaning and purpose that we find in familial relationships, friendships, exercises of moral and intellectual virtue, and engagements in intrinsically rewarding individual and collective pursuits does not – and, indeed, plausibly, cannot – depend upon what happens to the universe in the very distant future. The goods of the Aristotelian good life are *intrinsically* valuable: they are goods in themselves, and they remain goods in themselves even if they shall eventually have vanished without trace. Naturalists can certainly – and plausibly – deny that our lives have no meaning and no purpose merely because, if Naturalism is true, then it is very likely that human beings shall eventually vanish from the universe, and leave not a trace.

DOI: 10.1057/9781137354143

Perhaps it might be alleged that Naturalism entails that our lives have no meaning and no purpose because, if Naturalism is true, then there is no possibility of life after death. Here, we make the same reply as in the previous case. The meaning and purpose that we find in familial relationships, friendships, exercises of moral and intellectual virtue, and engagements in intrinsically rewarding individual and collective pursuits does not – and, indeed, plausibly, cannot – depend upon whether there is an afterlife. Even if – as Naturalists may well believe – it is *impossible* for there to be life after death, this does nothing to undermine the intrinsically valuable goods of the Aristotelian good life.

Perhaps it might be alleged that Naturalism entails that our lives have no meaning and no purpose because, if Naturalism is true, then there is no epic cosmic melodrama in which human beings feature as central characters. Here, again, we make the same kind of reply. The meaning and purpose that we find in familial relationships, friendships, exercises of moral and intellectual virtue, and engagements in intrinsically rewarding individual and collective pursuits does not – and, indeed, plausibly, cannot – depend upon whether there is an epic cosmic melodrama in which human beings feature as central characters. Even if – as Naturalists may well believe – it is *impossible* for there to be an epic cosmic melodrama in which human beings feature as central characters, this does nothing to undermine the intrinsically valuable goods of the Aristotelian good life.

Even if it is accepted that Naturalists are entitled to believe that our lives can have meaning and purpose even though the universe will experience heat death, and even though there is no life after death, and even though there is no epic cosmic melodrama in which human beings feature as central characters, it might nonetheless be said that Theism is to be preferred to Naturalism because Theism can be naturally expanded to accommodate the claims that there is life after death and that there is an epic cosmic melodrama in which human beings feature as central characters, and hence can be naturally expanded to attribute vastly more meaning and purpose to our lives. However, the proper response to this, I think, is that we are interested in assessing the comparative merits of Naturalism and Theism against the evidence that we have available to us. Whether considerations about life after death and epic cosmic melodramas featuring human beings as central characters favour Theism over Naturalism depends entirely upon whether there is evidence in favour of life after death and epic cosmic melodramas featuring human beings as central characters. But we have already seen that it is implausible to

DOI: 10.1057/9781137354143

claim that the available evidence does favour life after death and epic cosmic melodramas featuring human beings as central characters.

Hiddenness and non-belief

Suppose that you are persuaded by the argument to this point: the evidence that we have considered favours Naturalism over Theism, and it is unlikely that there is significant evidence that we have not yet taken into account. Then perhaps you might think that we have a further piece of evidence that works in favour of Naturalism over Theism: for isn't it more likely that our evidence will favour Naturalism over Theism if, in fact, Naturalism is true?

If there were an omnipotent, omniscient and perfectly good source, or ground, or originating cause of everything that can have a source, or ground, or originating cause, then perhaps we should expect – on account of God's omniscience and perfect goodness – that God would know about us and love us, and that, given other features of the world in which we live, that God should want to make his existence known to us. After all, it seems plausible to suppose that we ought to feel reassured by the thought that there is an omnipotent creator who cares about us. But, as we have just noted, the evidence that we have considered clearly does not unequivocally favour Theism over Naturalism – and, indeed, if the argument developed so far is correct, probably favours Naturalism over Theism. However, if the evidence that we have considered favours Naturalism over Theism – or even if the evidence that we have considered fails to favour Theism over Naturalism – then it seems that *that* is one more piece of evidence that favours Naturalism over Theism.

Perhaps it might be objected that God would have other, outweighing, reasons for not making his existence clearly known to all of us. On the one hand, it might be said that knowledge that God exists would interfere with our free deliberative capacities: in order to be able to encounter the kinds of serious moral choices that make our lives valuable, we must be placed in circumstances in which there is no unequivocal evidence that God exists. And, on the other hand, it might be said that there is no reason to expect that God's reasons for remaining hidden from us should be accessible to us: who are we to suppose that we have what it takes to fathom the divine mind?

DOI: 10.1057/9781137354143

The claim that the knowledge that God exists would interfere with our free deliberative capacities seems mistaken. Suppose that we do know that God exists: there is an omnipotent, omniscient and perfectly good source, or ground, or originating cause of everything that can have a source, or ground, or originating cause. Consider a serious moral question: say, whether we should permit first trimester abortion. How does our knowledge that there is an omnipotent, omniscient and perfectly good source, or ground, or originating cause of everything that can have a source, or ground, or originating cause constrain the range of views that we might adopt? As far as I can see, the answer to this question is: not at all! We can know that there is an omnipotent, omniscient and perfectly good source, or ground, or originating cause of everything that can have a source, or ground, or originating cause, and yet be completely in the dark about what that being wants us to do when faced with particular moral decisions! Of course, some theists will suppose that they have evidence about what God wants us to do in the face of particular moral decisions – but theists disagree enormously amongst themselves on a vast range of significant moral decisions.

The claim that there is no reason to expect that God's reasons for remaining hidden from us should be accessible to us does not look like a winning move in the context of the decision between Theism and Naturalism. On the one hand, data about absence of evidence for the existence of God and prevalence of non-belief in God have a ready explanation if Naturalism is true. On the other hand, the explanation that is now being offered on behalf of Theism is that God has reasons for not providing sufficient evidence for his existence to us, and for allowing reasonable non-belief to proliferate, but these reasons are not currently available to us (and may never be available to us). It is hard to believe that this is a more virtuous explanation than the ready explanation that is available to Naturalism.

Concluding remarks

We have considered the bearing of a wide range of evidence on (Standard) Theism and (Standard) Naturalism: the concept of God, global causal structure, cosmic fine-tuning, history of the earth, history of humanity, a priori knowledge, morality and human flourishing, consciousness and reason, religious experience, scripture, authority, organisation

DOI: 10.1057/9781137354143

and tradition, horrendous evil, salvation, meaning and purpose, hiddenness and non-belief. We began by observing that, apart from the consideration of evidence, (Standard) Naturalism has an advantage over (Standard) Theism, namely, that it is simpler: it postulates fewer and less complex primitive entities; it has fewer and less complex primitive features; it appeals to fewer and less complex primitive principles. We then noted that none of the evidence that we considered favoured (Standard) Theism over (Standard) Naturalism. The conclusion that we should draw is that, given the evidence that we have examined (Standard) Naturalism is to be preferred to (Standard) Theism.

References and further reading

On arguments from evil: John Mackie (1955) 'Evil and Omnipotence' *Mind* 64, 200–12; William Rowe (1979) 'The Problem of Evil and some Varieties of Atheism' *American Philosophical Quarterly* 16, 335–41; Daniel Howard-Snyder (ed.) (1996) *The Evidential Argument from Evil* Bloomington: Indiana University Press; Mark Larrimore (ed.) (2004) *The Problem of Evil: A Reader* Oxford: Blackwell; Bruce Langtry (2008) *God, the Best, and Evil* Oxford: Oxford University Press.

On Pascal's Wager: Jeff Jordan (ed.) (1994) *Gambling on God: Essays on Pascal's Wager* Lanham: Rowman & Littlefield. My favourite critique: Alan Hájek (2003) 'Waging War on Pascal's Wager' *Philosophical Review* 112, 27–56.

On meaning and purpose: E. D. Klemke (ed.) (2000) *The Meaning of Life*, second edition New York: Oxford University Press; Julian Baggini (2005) *What's It all about? Philosophy and the Meaning of Life* Oxford: Oxford University Press; Susan Wolf (2010) *Meaning in Life and Why It Matters* Princeton: Princeton University Press.

On hiddenness and non-belief: John Schellenberg (1993) *Divine Hiddenness and Human Reason* Ithaca: Cornell University Press; Ted Drange (1998) *Nonbelief and Evil: Two Arguments for the Non-Existence of God* Amherst: Prometheus; Daniel Howard-Snyder and Paul Moser (eds) (2001) *Divine Hiddenness: New Essays* Cambridge: Cambridge University Press.

DOI: 10.1057/9781137354143

Conclusion

Abstract: *We consider the prospects of turning the results of our comparison of Naturalism and Theism on selected data into a successful argument for Naturalism. We argue that there are good reasons for thinking that those prospects are dim: there are strong reasons for thinking that any such argument will be rationally resistible. We conclude with some very brief remarks about the role of faith in Theistic belief, and of the significance of our comparison of Naturalism and Theism on selected data for the rationality of Theistic belief.*

Keywords: Clifford; evidence; faith; James; judgement; rationality; reason

Oppy, Graham. *The Best Argument against God.*
Basingstoke: Palgrave Macmillan, 2013.
DOI: 10.1057/9781137354143.

Suppose you agree that, given the evidence that we have examined (Standard) Naturalism is to be preferred to (Standard) Theism. What follows?

Clearly enough – quite apart from the thought that there might be a mistake that we have made in our assessment of the evidence, or in the methods that we have used in assessing the comparative merits of Naturalism and Theism on that evidence – one might think that there might be further evidence, that we have not considered, that might make a difference to the outcome of our deliberations. In order to consider the implications of this observation, it is worth thinking about the argumentative strategy that has been employed so far.

We began, roughly, with the idea that, because Theism is an extension of Naturalism – Theism has all of the natural commitments that Naturalism has, but adds additional supernatural commitments to it – the most central question is whether there is some evidence that warrants those additional supernatural commitments. In particular, we have the idea that, if there is to be genuine evidential warrant to move beyond Naturalism, it must be that we have some evidence that is clearly better explained on Theism than it is on Naturalism.

The argument set out to this point claims that we have not found any evidence that is clearly better explained on Theism than on Naturalism. However, if there were such evidence – that is, if we found some evidence that is clearly better explained on Theism than on Naturalism – then it seems that all argumentative bets would be off. In particular, if there is some evidence that is better explained by Theism than by Naturalism – whether or not there is also some evidence that is better explained by Naturalism than by Theism – we would then face the difficulty of deciding whether the taking on of supernatural commitments is justified by the explanatory advantage afforded by the evidence in question. Because, as we noted initially, there is no algorithm that tells us how to evaluate that kind of trade-off, we might well think that it would then be simply a matter for judgment – and, perhaps, that it would then be a matter for judgment about which there can be reasonable disagreement.

Given that there is uncertainty about whether all relevant evidence has been canvassed, it seems that, even if we think that there is nothing else that has gone wrong in the preceding assessment, we should not be *too* confident that there is a compelling evidential argument in favour of Naturalism over Theism. Moreover, if we think that considerations about the difficulties involved in properly assessing *all* of the evidence

DOI: 10.1057/9781137354143

that might bear on the decision between Naturalism and Theism make us sceptical about the prospects of arriving at a decisive evidential argument, we might also reflect that this would hardly be an unexpected outcome.

After all, before we turn to considerations of evidence that bears on the decision between Naturalism and Theism, we *know* that there are millions of thoughtful, informed, reflective, intelligent people who occupy each of the views that it is possible to take: there are millions of thoughtful, informed, reflective, intelligent Theists; there are millions of thoughtful, informed, reflective, intelligent Naturalists; and there are millions of thoughtful, informed, reflective, intelligent people who are undecided between these two positions. Given just this data, we can be more or less certain that there is no simple range of considerations that decides between these positions: if there were a simple range of considerations that decisively favoured one of these positions, then it would be an almost inexplicable mystery why thoughtful, informed, intelligent, reflective opinion has not converged on that position. Moreover, given this data, we can be more or less certain that the decision between these positions is a matter for judgment – that is, a matter that cannot be compressed into an algorithmic computation; if the decision between these positions could be compressed into an algorithmic computation, then, again, it would be an almost inexplicable mystery why thoughtful, informed, intelligent, reflective opinion has not converged on that position, particularly given the amount of effort that has been invested in trying to carry out the relevant assessment.

Of course, the discussion to this point has been concerned only with an *evidential* assessment of the comparative merits of Theism and Naturalism. Even if we reached the view that all of the evidence that we have favours Naturalism over Theism, it is not clear that we could immediately go on to conclude that we are therefore rationally required to prefer Naturalism to Theism. For, it might be said, we might have non-evidential reasons to prefer Theism to Naturalism, and those non-evidential reasons might outweigh whatever evidential advantage Naturalism enjoys.

Opinions about *faith* – believing what the evidence fails to say is so – vary. On the one hand, there are those who insist that it is simply irrational to hold beliefs that run beyond one's evidence: if the evidence that we have fails to favour Theism over Naturalism, then it would simply be irrational to espouse Theism. On the other hand, there are those who

DOI: 10.1057/9781137354143

insist that, at least in the case where the evidence is indecisive, it can be perfectly rational to hold beliefs that run beyond one's evidence.

William Clifford (1845–79) is perhaps the best-known standard-bearer for the view that, if the evidence that we have fails to favour Theism over Naturalism, then it would simply be irrational to espouse Theism. Clifford insists that it is irrational, always, everywhere, for anyone, to believe anything on insufficient evidence. Hence, in particular, Clifford is plainly committed to the view that it is irrational, always, everywhere, for anyone, to believe a theory which does not receive more support from all of the available evidence than some competing theory. In fact, Clifford goes even further: he thinks that it is also *morally wrong*, always, everywhere, for anyone, to believe a theory which does not receive more support from all of the available evidence than some competing theory. (See W. Clifford 'The Ethics of Belief' in *Lectures and Essays*, edited by S. Pollock, London: Macmillan, 1879, 177–87.)

William James is one well-known standard-bearer for the view that, even if the evidence that we have fails to favour Theism over Naturalism, it may nonetheless be perfectly rational to espouse Theism. Indeed, James claims that 'our passional nature not only lawfully may, but must, decide an option between propositions whenever it is a genuine option that cannot by its nature be decided on intellectual grounds'. Against Clifford, James claims that there need be no epistemic or moral wrong involved in believing a theory which does not receive more support from all of the available evidence than some competing theory. (See W. James 'The Will to Believe' in *The Will to Believe and Other Essays in Popular Philosophy*, New York: Longmans, Green, and Co., 1912, 2–30.)

We shall not attempt to adjudicate the dispute to which Clifford and James are parties. Such adjudication would be a major undertaking, and goes well beyond the brief of the present work. The point to take away is just that, even if it is true that the evidence does not favour (Standard) Theism over (Standard) Naturalism – or Theism over Naturalism, or theism over naturalism – there is no clear, immediate and uncontested consequence that follows concerning the *rationality* of acceptance of (Standard) Theism, or Theism, or theism.

DOI: 10.1057/9781137354143

Index

Al-Hijira, 63
Allah, 80
alternative medicine, 36
ancestral spirits, 5
angel, 76
anomalous phenomena,
    36, 56
Anselm, 20
antikythera mechanism, 32
a priori knowledge, 38
Aquinas, St. Thomas, 24
▶ argument, 8
Aristotle, 81
Arunagirinathar, 36
Asala, 63
Atheism, 6
Australia, 48
authority, 62
Avesta, 62

Behe, Michael, 34
belief, 76
Beopheung of Silla,
    King, 36
Bhagavad-Gita, 62
Bible, 62
Britannica Year Book, 48
Buddha, 36, 62

Carroll, Lewis, 41, 58
causal determinism, 14
causal reality, 6
cause, 13
Chalmers, David, 53
chance, 12

Christianity, 5
Christmas, 63
Clifford, William, 90
cognitive bias, 49
compatibilism, 15, 73
conclusion, 9
Confucius, 62
conscience, 45
consciousness, 52, 54
contingency, 13
cosmic fine-tuning, 27
cosmological argument from
    contingency, 26

decision rule, 79
demon, 76
Denmark, 48
Descartes, René, 38
Devil, 76
*Dialogues Concerning Natural
    Religion*, 19
divine attribute, 5
divine commands, 16
divine grace, 75
divine hiddenness, 84
Diwali, 63

Easter, 63
ecstasy, 60
encounter, 60
Epicurus, 72, 74
Epistles of Wisdom, 62
Ethics, 81
Euclid, 40
Euthyphro, 44

evidence of non-belief, 84
explanatory breadth, 8

faith, 89
Fátima, 36
fictionalism, 41
Five Classics, 62
Four Books, 62
freedom, 15

Gaunilo, 21
Geoghan, John, 48
Ghanghra river, 36
global causal structure, 23
God, 5, 76
Goodness of Fit, 8
greatest possible being, 19

Hadith, 62
Haggard, Ted, 48
Hannukah, 63
happiness, 51
hard determinism, 15
Heaven, 75
Hell, 75
Hinduism, 5
Hola Mohalla, 63
Holi, 63
hope, 76
horrendous suffering, 68
human flourishing, 43
Hume, David, 19, 37

Ichadon, 36
imagination, 12
Imhotep, 62
incompatibilism, 15
inference, 57
infinity of primes, 40
interactive substance dualism, 57
intrinsic maximum, 22
Ireland, 48
Islam, 5

James, William, 60, 77, 90
Jamshedi Noruz, 63
Jesus, 36, 62, 80

Judaism, 5

kalâm cosmological argument, 26
Khordad Sal, 63
Kohler, Wolfgang, 42
Kojiki, 62
Krishna, 62

Lao-Tzu, 62
Laplace, Pierre de, 30, 35
Leibniz, Gottfried, 53
libertarianism, 15, 73
life after death, 83
logic, 38

mathematics, 38
meaning, 81
metaphysics, 38
Method, 7
miracle, 36, 56
mixed strategy, 79
modality, 38
Mohammed, 36, 62, 80
Monadology, 53
Monotheism, 5
morality, 16, 43
moral knowledge, 45
moral responsibility, 16
moral truth, 43
Moses, 62

Naturalism, 6
Naturalist, 9
natural reality, 6
natural science, 30
Natural Theology, 32
necessary cause, 14
necessity, 13
nominalism, 41
numinosity, 60

objectivity, 16
OHair, Madelyn Murray, 48
omnibenevolence, 5
omnipotence, 5
omniscience, 5
organisation, 62

DOI: 10.1057/9781137354143

Otto, Rudolf, 60

Paley's 'Watch' argument, 32
Paley, William, 32
Pali Canon, 62
Pascal, Blaise, 77
Pellicer, Miguel Juan, 36
Pensées, 77
Plato, 44
Platonism, 41
Politics, 81
Polytheism, 5
possession, 60
possibility, 12
Predictive Fruitfulness, 8
premise, 9
primitive features, 6
primitive property, 55
Proslogion II, 20
pure strategy, 79
purpose, 81

quantum mechanics, 14
Quran, 62

Ramadan, 63
rat lungworm larvae, 53
reason, 52, 57
reductio ad absurdum, 23
religious experience, 59
Ridvan, 63
Russell, Bertrand, 48

Samhain, 63
Santo, Audrey Marie, 36
Sarkar Waris Pak, 36
Satkhandagama, 62
scope of possibility, 12
scripture, 62
Second Way, 24
sense of oneness, 60
Shogatsu, 63
Shubun-sai, 63
Simplicity, 7
social science, 35
societal dysfunction, 47, 52

source of infinite value, 80
Stalin, Josef, 48
statistics, 38
stereotypes, 49
structuralism, 41
sufficient cause, 14
Summa Theologiae, 24
Sunnah, 62
Supernaturalism, 6
support, 9
Swaggart, Jimmy, 48
System 1/System 2, 58, 61

Talmud, 62
Tanakh, 62
Tao Te Ching, 62
the five pillars, 75
The Idea of the Holy, 60
Theism, 5
Theist, 9
The Mentality of Apes, 42
the noble eightfold path, 75
theoretical virtues, 7
The Varieties of Religious
    Experience, 60
tradition, 62
Trinity, 5

United States, 48
unity, 60
Upanishads, 62

Vaisakhi, 63
Vedas, 62
vice, 49
virtue, 47

Wesak, 63
Wikipedia, 48

yoga, 75
Yom Kippur, 63
Yule, 63

zombie, 53
Zoroaster, 62

DOI: 10.1057/9781137354143